T0047073

The School of Life:
A Job to Love

First published in 2017 by The School of Life
First published in the USA in 2018
This paperback edition published in 2023
930 High Road, London, N12 9RT
Copyright © The School of Life 2023

Designed and typeset by Marcia Mihotich
Printed and bound in Canada

A proportion of this book has appeared online at www.theschooloflife.com/articles

Every effort has been made to contact the copyright holders of the material reproduced in this book. If any have been inadvertently overlooked, the publisher will be pleased to make restitution at the earliest opportunity.

The School of Life publishes a range of books on essential topics in psychological and emotional life, including relationships, parenting, friendship, careers, and fulfillment. The aim is always to help us to understand ourselves better—and thereby to grow calmer, less confused, and more purposeful. Discover our full range of titles, including books for children, here: www.theschooloflife.com/books

The School of Life also offers a comprehensive therapy service, which complements, and draws upon, our published works: www.theschooloflife.com/therapy

www.theschooloflife.com

ISBN 978-1-915087-31-7

10 9 8 7 6 5 4 3 2 1

The School of Life:
A Job to Love

How to find a fulfilling career

The School of Life

Introduction

Introduction

i. How We Came to Desire a Job We Could Love

One of the most extraordinary and yet quietly routine features of our age is the assumption that we should be able to find work that we not only tolerate, or endure for the money, but profoundly appreciate for its high degree of purpose, camaraderie, and creativity. We see nothing strange in the remarkable notion that we should try to find a job we love.

It is possible to be highly sympathetic to this wish and yet refuse to see it as either normal or easy to fulfill and to insist that, in order to stand any chance of honoring it, we need to lavish concentrated brain power, time, and imagination on its underlying complexities.

For most of history, the question of whether we might love our work would have seemed laughable or peculiar. We tilled the soil and herded animals, worked down mines and emptied chamber pots. And we suffered. The serf or smallholder could look forward to only a very few moments of satisfaction, and these would lie firmly outside the hours of employment: the harvest moon festival next year or the wedding day of their eldest child, currently 6 years old.

The corresponding assumption was that if we had sufficient money, we would simply stop working. The educated classes among the ancient Romans (whose attitudes dominated Europe for centuries) considered all paid work to be inherently humiliating. Tellingly, their word for business was *negotium*: literally, "not-enjoyable activity." Leisure, doing not very much, perhaps hunting or giving dinner parties, was felt to be the sole basis for a life of happiness.

Then, at the close of the Middle Ages, an extraordinary shift began: a few people started to work for money and for fulfillment. One of the first people to successfully pursue this highly unusual ambition was the Venetian artist Titian (c. 1485–1576). On the one hand, in his work he delighted in the pleasures of creativity: depicting the way light fell on a sleeve or unlocking the secret of a friend's smile. But he added something very odd to this: He was extremely interested in being paid well. He was highly astute when it came to negotiating contracts for supplying pictures, and he upped his output (and profit margin) by establishing a factory system of assistants who specialized in different phases of the production process, such as painting drapery (he hired five young men from Verona to paint the curtains in his work). He was one of the initiators of a profound new idea: that work could and should be both something you love doing and a decent source of income. This was a revolutionary idea that gradually spread across the world. Nowadays it reigns supreme, coloring our ambitions perhaps without us even noticing, and helping to define the hopes and frustrations of an accountant in Baltimore or a game designer in Limehouse.

Titian introduced a complicating factor into the modern psyche. Previously, you either pursued satisfaction making or doing something as an amateur without expecting to make money from your efforts, or you worked for money and didn't care too much about whether you actually enjoyed your work. Now, because of the new ideology of work, neither was quite acceptable any longer. The two ambitions—money and inner fulfillment—were being asked to coalesce. Good work meant, essentially, work that tapped into the deepest parts of the self and could generate a product or service that would pay for one's material needs. This dual demand has ushered in a particular difficulty of modern life: that we must simultaneously pursue two very complicated ambitions, although these are far from inevitably aligned. We need to satisfy the soul and pay for our material existence.

Interestingly, it's not just around the ideal of a job that we have developed high ambitions that combine the spiritual and the material. Something very similar has happened around relationships. For the largest part of human history, it would have been extraordinary to suppose that one was meant to love (rather than merely tolerate) one's spouse. The point of marriage was inherently practical: uniting adjacent plots of land, finding someone who would be good at milking cows or who might bear a brood of healthy children. Romantic love was something distinct—it might be nice for one summer when one was 15, or might be pursued with someone other than one's spouse after the birth of the seventh child. Then, in around 1750, a peculiar shift began to take place here as well. We started to be interested in another extraordinarily ambitious idea: a marriage of love. A new kind of hope started to obsess people: that one could both be married and properly admire and sympathize with one's partner. Instead of there being two distinct projects—marriage and love—a new and more complex ideal emerged: the marriage of passion.

The modern world is built around hopeful visions of how things that had previously seemed separate (money and creative fulfillment; love and marriage) could be united. These are generous ideas, democratic in spirit, filled with optimism about what we can achieve, and rightfully intolerant of ancient forms of suffering. But in the way we have tried to act upon them, they have also been catastrophes. They constantly let us down. They breed impatience and feelings of paranoia and persecution. They generate powerful new ways of being frustrated. We judge our lives by ambitious new standards by which we are continually made to feel we have fallen short.

It's an added complication that, although we have set ourselves such impressive goals, we have tended to tell ourselves that the way to attain them is not essentially difficult. It is just a case, we assume, of following our instincts. We'll find the right relationship (which unites passion with day-to-day practical stability) and a good career (which unites the practical goal of earning an income with a sense of inner fulfillment) by following our feelings. We trust that we'll just develop a special kind of emotional rush in the presence of the right person or will, once we've finished college, sense a reliable pull towards a career that is right for us. We put a decisive share of our trust in the phenomenon of gut instinct.

A symptom of our devotion to instinct is that we don't readily recognize much need for training and education around getting into a relationship or in the search for a career. We take it for granted, for instance, that children will need many hundreds of hours of carefully considered instruction if they are to become competent at math or learn a foreign language. We understand that instinct and luck can't ever lead to good results in chemistry—and that it would be cruel to suppose otherwise. But we'd think it odd if the school curriculum included an almost daily strand over many years of classes on how to make a relationship work or how to find a job that accorded with one's talents and interests. We may recognize that these decisions are hugely important and consequential, yet by a strange quirk of intellectual history we've come to suppose that they can't be taught or educated for. They really matter, but we seem to believe that the right answer will just float into our brains when the moment is ripe.

The aim of The School of Life is to correct such unwittingly cruel assumptions, and to equip us with ideas with which to better accomplish the admirable (but in truth highly difficult) ambitions that we harbor around our emotional and working lives.

ii. How Alone We Are on Our Search

Several obstacles typically stand in the way of finding a fulfilling job. Some of these have been well understood already, and established institutions are in place to help us overcome them.

1. A lack of skills

It's long been understood that many fulfilling jobs require you to possess a particular range of skills and specialist ideas. You might need to be able to juggle landing slots confidently or negotiate in the East Asian language of a key group of international clients; you might need detailed knowledge of the anatomy of the inner ear or the tensile properties of concrete. So, over time, schools, universities, and technical colleges have emerged as places where the obstacles created by professional ignorance can in large part be addressed. We have become adept at facing the problems created by a lack of skills.

2. A lack of information about opportunities

It has not always been easy to know where the good jobs might lie. For much of history, people had no way of easily understanding where to look for openings. You could have been the ideal gamekeeper for an estate in a different state, but would never end up in the role for the banal but immovable reason that you'd never even heard there was such a position on offer. You might have had the perfect temperament and qualifications for running a new cotton mill, but if you didn't happen to know a friend of a friend, your career as a lock keeper would have continued without relief until the end. This fateful issue too has now been well identified and addressed. We've invented a plethora of employment and recruitment agencies, headhunting firms and networking sites, together ensuring that we can pretty much be guaranteed to have sound insights into where the demand for different forms of labor might lie.

3. A lack of a coherent goal

But one major obstacle to finding a suitable job remains, and it is one that has received much less attention than the other two, even if it is the most important of them all: the painful challenge of working out what kind of job we are well suited for and would love to do. Not knowing what we seek is simply the most important of the three hurdles: without it, education and market opportunities do not deliver on their promises.

To address this problem, we have collectively invented surprisingly little. We do give it some attention, of course. Schools and colleges prompt students to sit down with a counselor and mull over the question for an hour or two; and we're likely to run across some kinds of diagnostic tests intended to steer us towards career options that might suit our personalities. Many of these are based on the Myers–Briggs questionnaire, originally developed in the first half of the 20th century.

Such a test is likely to involve hundreds of multiple-choice questions, many of which ask one to rate occupations such as "working outdoors" or "helping others in a retail environment" with terms ranging from "not interested" to "strong preference." The underlying intention is very benign. Such tests seek to identify our personality types, of which there are, classically, 16 options, ranging from ISTJ (introverted with strengths in sensing, thinking, and judgment) to ENFP (extroverted with strengths of intuition, feeling, and perceiving)—and then align us with work where these characteristics could be of optimal value.

However, as we currently know them, these diagnostic exercises have some extremely important and interesting shortcomings. They might feel quite long— you could spend up to an hour doing one—but given the weight of the overarching question (how to find a good career), this might actually be far too brief. Furthermore, they tend to be vague and detached in the guidance they offer. They might alert us to the fact that we are strongly creative but score less highly on the rational indicators, or that we could thrive in a team leadership role or in a position with customers, but they don't home in on the details of our particular individual capacities. We might be steered towards an oddly open-ended array of career options: Our answers indicate that we might be suited to working with animals or in a job involving numbers.

We can get a sense of how inadequate current provisions are by considering some of the people with the most fulfilling careers in history, and trying to imagine what the current test providers might have advised them to do. Suppose Mozart had done a Myers–Briggs test. Once he'd submitted his responses, he might have received a version of this kind of advice: "Your optimal work position involves working imaginatively with ideas or designs. This includes jobs in the arts, performing, creative writing and also visual design, lateral thinking, business creativity, adapting or coming up with new ideas and working in situations where no rulebook exists. Example jobs include: graphic designer, training consultant, wedding planner, public relations." That's very far from *Don Giovanni* or the Clarinet Concerto in A Major.

The absurdity shows how removed many tests are from being able to direct an individual with any level of seriousness or focus. The more fulfilling the career, the more the current style of exercise looks incongruous and ineffective.

Truly useful career advice for Mozart would have needed to be more specific: having taken an ideal test, which probed the really crucial parts of his personality, strengths and deficiencies, he would have been offered guidance such as: "Take the contrapuntal complexities of late Baroque cantatas, simplify them and extend their emotional range; try to collaborate with a witty, but philosophically minded, librettist; your results suggest you are particularly suited to integrating comic or ironic elements into solemn and grand situations. Focus your remorse and anxiety about death in writing a requiem. Overall goal: reorient the course of Western musical culture."

Such limitations don't arise only in the rare case of geniuses. It would not be a major problem if a job aptitude test did not do perfect justice to 0.1 percent of the population. But a more troubling, yet more accurate, thought is that a huge quantity of human talent of very high caliber remains inadequately developed because of a lack of good advice and guidance at crucial moments. The failure to receive genuinely well-targeted counsel affects us all—even if we can usefully recognize the deficiency first in extreme cases such as that of Mozart. A great many people are vaguely, and not inaccurately, haunted by the idea that they could in principle do something properly world changing, although they can't put their finger on what or how. We are in drastic need of richer sources of guidance.

The English poet Thomas Gray (1716–1771) meditated on the melancholy theme of unexploited talent while looking at the headstones of farm laborers in the graveyard of a small country village. He wondered who these people had been and what, in better circumstances, they might have become:

Perhaps in this neglected spot is laid
Some heart once pregnant with celestial fire;

Hands, that the rod of empire might have sway'd,
Or waked to ecstasy the living lyre.
…
Full many a flower is born to blush unseen,
And waste its sweetness on the desert air.
…
Some mute inglorious Milton here may rest

Thomas Gray, 'Elegy Written in a Country
Churchyard' (1751)

Gray's elegantly expressed thought is genuinely disturbing and, in a sense, an outrage: With the right opportunities and guidance, so-called ordinary people are capable of major contributions to existence.

Today, the obstacles aren't just about a lack of education or an inability to identify where the opportunities might lie: They comprise a failure to arrive at accurate analyses of our capacities and guidance about how to develop these. This is the tantalizing ideal that career diagnostic tests currently only gesture towards from a great distance.

One special problem with today's tests is that they stick rigidly to kinds of work that already exist. This isn't surprising—the tests originated at a time when the job market was relatively stable and career options were generally clearly defined. But it's eminently possible that the kind of work someone is best suited to (and around which it will be possible for them to love what they do) doesn't exist yet. One might have a great deal of potential for a kind of job that has yet to be invented.

If, in 1925, the 36-year-old James O. McKinsey had taken the recently invented Myers–Briggs test, it would have revealed his strong intellectual and problem-solving aptitudes. The job suggestions might have focused on academia (in fact, he had recently been appointed as a professor) or a career in industry. What it wouldn't have done was to steer him towards the thing he was actually going to be very good at: integrating the two. It would not have suggested to him that he search for a new kind of work, hitherto unnamed. He would have been alone in his search. In his case, things worked out well for him: the next year, he founded McKinsey & Company and initiated the idea of management consultancy, which (at its occasional best) helpfully brings together research and practical decision-making. Inadvertently, tests like the Myers–Briggs—with their suggestions of ideal jobs based on existing categories—edge us away from what might actually be the most interesting line we could pursue.

We should not blame ourselves for our confusions. Our culture has set us a difficult problem: promising us that fulfilling jobs exist while leaving us woefully unprepared for how to discover our own aptitudes and appetites. The purpose of this book is to help to correct an epochal problem that quietly gnaws at our lives and tramples upon our legitimate hopes.

1

Obstacles to Having Goals

i. The "Vocation Myth"

The difficulty of defining a professional goal may be both serious and widespread, but it currently lacks the generous, extensive, and careful consideration it deserves. In truth, we tend to see confusion about our career paths as a slightly embarrassing failing that reflects poorly on its sufferers. Confusion is readily taken as a sign of being a bit muddled and impractical, of being unreasonably picky or hard to please. We might regard it as a consequence of being spoilt ("you should be thankful for any job") or as a troubling symptom of a lack of commitment or general flightiness. We arrive at these rather harsh assessments because we're still under the spell of a big and often poisonous idea that can be termed the "vocation myth".

This myth originated around certain religious experiences, which, although rare, were regarded as hugely impressive and significant—and were accorded an inordinate degree of publicity in the history of the West. These were moments when an individual was summoned by God—sometimes speaking through an angel, at other points talking directly through the clouds—and directed to devote their life to an aspect of the divine cause.

One significant story concerned the philosopher St Augustine (354–430 CE), who, in midlife, changed jobs under divine instruction. He went from being a pagan professor of literature to being a Catholic bishop. It was a huge career change, but Augustine didn't have to work it out on his own. In 386 CE, he happened to be staying in Milan and one day went out for a walk. He heard a child singing a lovely song he'd never heard before. The words of the chorus were "pick it up, pick it up," which he understood as a command from God. He was to pick up a Bible and read the first passage he set his eyes on— and the very one he alighted upon told him to change his life and become the figure we know today as the great Catholic thinker and clergyman.

However tied to Catholic theology the story might seem, we have secularized such accounts without quite realizing it. We too proceed as if at some point we might expect to hear a quasicelestial command directing us towards our life's purpose.

It started—as often happens—with artists. Up until the Renaissance, being an artist was just a kind of job that some people had, almost always because it was something that their father or uncle was involved in. Being a painter or making statues wasn't regarded as radically different from making shoes or bridles for horses: It was just a useful skilled trade that any assiduous individual who went through the proper course of training could become good at with time. But then, borrowing from the religious stories, artists began to think of themselves as "called" by fate to a particular line of work. Something within them was pulling them towards their art. Michelangelo (1475–1564) was the most extreme example of this attitude, believing that his soul required him to paint fresco ceilings and chip away at blocks of marble. He might at times have wished he could stop, but to do so would have betrayed his vocation.

The notion of vocation features in the biographies of many of the world's most famous people. For example, we learn that the pioneering Polish scientist Marie Curie (1867–1934) knew from the age of 15 that her life depended on being able to undertake scientific research. She struggled determinedly against every difficulty in her path—she had no money and when she was a student she nearly froze to death one winter and frequently fainted from hunger. But eventually she triumphed and was awarded two Nobel prizes, the first in 1903 for her work on X-rays and the second in 1911 for the discovery of radium and polonium.

As a result of such cases, having a vocation has come to seem like a sure sign of being destined for great things. And, necessarily, to lack a vocation has come to seem not only a misfortune, but also a mark of inferiority. We end up not only panicked that we don't have a path in mind, but also dispirited that our ignorance is proof that any path we do end up on will necessarily be an insignificant one.

What is worse, "finding one's vocation" has come to seem like a discovery of which we should all be capable in a brief span of time. And the way to discover such a vocation should be (thanks to religious and artistic forerunners) entirely passive: We should simply wait for a moment of revelation, for the modern equivalent of a clap of thunder or a divine voice, an inner urge or an instinct pushing us towards podiatry or supply-chain management.

A small but significant echo of this attitude can be traced in our habit of asking even very young children what they want to be when they grow up. There's a faint but revealing assumption that somewhere in the options being entertained by the child (footballer, zookeeper, space explorer, etc.), there will already be the first stumbling articulations of the crucial inner voice announcing the small person's true destiny. It appears not to strike us as peculiar to expect a 5-and-a-half-year-old to understand their identity in the adult labor market.

All this helps to explain the relative societal silence around the task of working out what to do. Well-meaning friends and family will often simply advise a confused person to wait: One day, something will strike them as just right.

Of course, contrary to what this unfortunate, oppressive notion of vocation suggests, it is entirely reasonable—even healthy—not to know what one's talents are or how to apply them. Our natures are so complex, our abilities so tricky to define in detail, the needs of the world so elusive, that discovering the best fit between ourselves and a job is a momentous, highly legitimate challenge that requires an immense amount of thought, exploration, and wise assistance and might use up years of our attention. It's wholly reasonable not to know what work we should perform. And it is indeed often a great sign of maturity to realize that we don't know, rather than suffer any longer under the punishing assumption that we should.

ii. The Vagueness of Our Minds

Even when we accept that working out what to do is something we'll need to devote much attention to over many years, we come up against a further, and much more puzzling, problem: how difficult it is to know the nature of our own minds.

Our brains are fatefully badly equipped to interpret and understand themselves. We cannot sit down and simply enquire of ourselves directly what we might want to do with our working lives—in the way we might ask ourselves what we would favor eating. The "we" retires, falls silent, and fragments under examination. At best, our deeper minds let out staccato signals as to certain things that appeal to, or appal them. We might find ourselves saying: "I want to do something creative" or "I don't want to give up my life to a corporation"; "I'd like to make a difference" or "I want meaningful work."

Such aspirations may be reasonable, but they are also foolhardy in their lack of definition. The prospect of having to build a career on their foundations can rightly induce panic; not having a robust plan swiftly puts us at the mercy of the plans of others. We're liable to blame ourselves and what seem like our exceptionally obtuse minds. But our incapacities are not unique. We're simply encountering—at an especially stressful moment—a basic problem of the human organ of thought. Our minds do not surrender answers to direct questions very easily. The same fractured replies would emerge if someone were to demand that we tell them what love really is or what friendship constitutes. We might feel baffled and put upon. We most probably wouldn't be able to come up with remotely sensible analyses, despite one striking and central fact: We are bound to have a lot of ideas lurking somewhere about the constitution of love and friendship, for we have all lived through plenty of their examples.

We already possess an immense amount of relevant material for framing extensive and highly penetrating insights. We've had so many fleeting thoughts and sensations; we've known situations both good and bad that could feed into profound responses. Yet somehow our experiences are too easily blocked from coalescing into robust replies. The problem is that our ideas have too often been left scattered in our minds. We haven't been able to collect them, sift through them, and see their connections and evolutions; we haven't had the time or encouragement to consider what each one is telling us and how they all stack up together. And yet, if we felt more intellectually dextrous and confident, we would all have the capacity to come up with perspectives of superlative value (the people we call great writers are in the end merely people who've known how to manipulate the butterfly nets required to catch their own flightiest, airiest, shyest thoughts).

There are so many things we already know without knowing that we know them—because we haven't been trained in the art of gathering and interpreting our experiences. What is a beautiful city like? What is an ideal vacation? How does a good conversation flow? The questions may sound daunting, but we have answers to them already—for we all harbor, somewhere within our memories, recollections of well-being as we walked the streets of a capital, or felt our senses reopen in a new climate, or registered our sympathies expanding at a table of friends. Our belief that we don't know is merely a symptom of tendencies to systematically underrate our own capacities.

With touching regularity, we dismiss the fact that we already contain within ourselves the power to address the grandest themes of existence.

Instead, from fear and habit, we turn away from inner exploration and reach for platitudes that we suspect won't do justice to our impressions, sensing that our real feelings are hiding somewhere in tangled preverbal form, yet hoping that our questioner might leave us and make someone else feel inadequate.

So there's ultimately nothing very special (and therefore nothing especially worrying) about our inability to give a direct or neat answer to an enquiry about what we might want to do with our working lives. It's merely one more example of our minds' unjustly weak and underconfident self-reflexive muscle.

Because our minds do not easily arrive at career plans, and yet the material for such plans is often in them, we should take the time to consciously collect relevant evidence, create a library for it, pore over it and analyze it, and so ensure that stray thoughts and fleeting sensory impressions can one day be assembled into clear propositions. There may be a few complexities to doing so (we will address them in a minute), but the chief obstacle to getting started is the melancholy feeling that it would be peculiar and unnecessary even to do so. A search to understand our working characters has to begin with a basic acknowledgment of the natural vagueness and intellectual squeamishness of our minds— without our falling prey to a sense that our furtive mental inclinations are shameful or indicative of any sort of individual weakness.

When addressing the question of what we might do in our work, we should have the confidence to believe that large portions of a sound answer are already going to be inside us. But the best way to proceed is not to try to head for a conclusion too quickly, because the data that can contribute to a reply usually hasn't been correctly studied or tagged within us; it doesn't know its own nature or its potential to guide us and has to be disentangled from cobwebs of error and forgetfulness. We must patiently trust that we have already picked up a great deal of information and experience relevant to determining what kind of work we should do, but that it has arrived in guises we won't automatically recognize or understand. Insofar as it is there, the information may just be encoded in those superlative indicators of career aptitude: distinctive feelings of pleasure, enthusiasm, or distaste in relation to many rather minor tasks and challenges—that can appear to be wholly disconnected from anything resembling a fee-paying job.

Paradoxically, it's not our direct past thoughts about work that are typically most useful in guiding us to new, more fulfilling, work. Our search is for work we can love, not work we have done—and so we need to get to know a lot about what we love and why before we move too quickly to the formulation of a career plan. We might begin by zeroing in on that storehouse of incidental career insights: childhood. When during these long years did we feel particular tremors of excitement? We should let our minds relax and surrender the smallest, most incidental, details.

Perhaps it was lovely lying on the bedroom floor in the old house (we must have been 8), cutting out pieces of paper from a colored pad and arranging alternating strips. Sometimes you used to particularly like just drawing straight lines across a blank piece of paper. Perhaps there was a sweater you especially responded to—it had yellow circles on the front; or you really liked running round some gorse bushes in the garden of a hotel you sometimes stayed at when you were little; or it was very special when your bedroom was extremely tidy. It was awful (maybe) at school when you had to do a joint project and your designated collaborator wouldn't accept your ideas about the size and shape of the presentation document, or about the order of the slides. Or you hated the way some people always kept their hair carefully brushed, or you loved the time you chatted with a friend about a fantasy desert island.

In such memories, we pick up on key incidents in the history of our intimate feelings. Something—we might not know exactly what—struck us as lovely or distressing. These very modest fragments hint at major tendencies in our nature that are liable to be still active within us, but not at an operative level. We will have to proceed slowly. It might take many months of careful reflection to uncover and define some of the central ingredients of our characters that can eventually function as important guides to a good working life.

It's not only the past that we need to investigate. We should also start to collect and analyze our sensations in the present. Because the mind is so prone to wiping out its own nascent autobiography every few hours, we should keep a notebook handy so we can trap a feeling and return to it later, attempting to make connections with other experiences we have registered. We should proceed with some of the patience of an ornithologist lying in the heather waiting for a sighting of a rare migrating bird.

The people who have perhaps most adroitly pioneered a careful method of data collection have been writers. Almost all of these types have kept notebooks, not because of how much they felt (constant sensations are universal), but because of how valuable they understood their apparently minor thoughts might be—and how aware they were of the cost of our brains' amnesiac tendencies.

The great French novelist Honoré de Balzac (1799–1850) was an inveterate notebook scribe. He was fascinated by human character, particularly by how the way people move and the expressions they exhibit give away key things about their personalities. With this theme in view, he became a constant observer of the mannerisms of people he saw in the streets of Paris or met at dinners and in offices. His notebooks tell us:

> *"Her movements are not equally distributed over her whole person; she advances in a single block at each step like the statue."*

> *"He walks like a despot: a menacing suggestion of security and strength in his slightest movements."*

> *"A brusque movement betrays a vice."*

> *"The way this woman saunters around, she can flaunt it all while revealing nothing."*

But Balzac didn't stop there. These moments of experience couldn't really honor their role until he worked out where they would be useful. In his case, this meant finding them a place in one of his stories. Although this concern might seem localized, he was stumbling upon a task that is really for everyone. We too need to trap and analyze our sensations, assembling from a thousand diverse hints the material that will form not so much a work of fiction but something far more important: the fabric of our own future working lives.

Exercise

The idea of finding our vocation suggests that we should, by now, know what job is right for us. Yet a more promising starting point is to acknowledge that we do not know at all.

The challenge is to get back in touch with our authentic desires. Oddly, these are often to be found in a time when we largely had no thought of work: childhood. Childhood is a good place to start because we pursued things then without many of the elements that later inhibit or distort interests. As children, we had no thought of status, money, or even whether we were any good at what we were doing. It can be valuable therefore to investigate childhood moments of enjoyment.

Step 1
Remember three things you enjoyed doing as a child.

- Describe the physical places where you used to play.
- What was it like to be in your room on a rainy day, or in the garden or yard?
- What would you do there?

Step 2
Write a few lines describing each of the three activities. For example, "I used to go downstairs and build a fort out of Lego. I sat in the middle of the floor, and I would

arrange all the pieces in order before I started." Or: "I used to pretend I was running an airline; I would transport food from the kitchen to my bedroom, and line up my soft toy animals to make announcements, as the captain."

Step 3

Imagine you are explaining to someone else why you loved doing this thing. Close your eyes and remember doing the activity. Describe the best moments.

What I particularly enjoyed was:
- when the houses were all lined up
- when the animals had been fed
- when we fell in the pool
- when I could instruct the passengers.

Now look behind these particular moments, to identify the underlying enjoyments of which these are one instance.

I enjoyed this because:
- creating a little orderly world is satisfying
- it's fun when you've made an animal happy
- I felt safe being with my friends
- I liked feeling I was in charge.

Step 4

Further elaborate your answers into descriptions of your inclinations:

- I'm someone who likes ... when there is order.
- I'm someone who likes ... making others happy.
- I'm someone who likes ... getting along with a team.
- I'm someone who likes ... when I'm in charge.

As children, we don't analyze our enjoyments, but it is often only as children that we get an intense, direct sense of our pleasures. Then we enter the desert of adolescence, when playfulness tends to become subordinated to the search for social success—and, eventually, to fitting into the economy. We arrive in adulthood with the thought of what might truly please us very far down our list of priorities.

This process above, which we should repeat for other childhood memories, helps us to get more specific about what we were enjoying when we were free to play as we liked. In this way we can build up a picture of what brings us joy, and therefore what work might satisfy us. A satisfying job will, in subtle, indirect but key ways, almost inevitably carry echoes of pleasures already known from childhood.

So far we've been collecting feelings. But there is a next step. We need to connect and generalize outwards from these feelings—while keeping in mind that their implications are almost always indirect. For example, the pleasure of reading a magazine shouldn't be taken to imply that we must try to work for a magazine. Our satisfactions deserve to be examined more closely in order to accurately reveal the real range of options before us. When they are attended to properly, the sensations around magazine reading typically contain hints of interests in careers that extend far beyond consumer publishing. It might be that we are drawn to something about the paper stock, or the pictures of interiors, or the tone in the problem pages, or an atmosphere of dynamism in the message from the editor that promises to compensate for a gap in our own background. These pleasures might have occurred while reading a magazine, but they are not necessarily especially tied to magazines. Our initial analysis may pass too swiftly over the real import of our sensations and can lead us in dangerously false directions. Although the information relevant for guiding us just happened to manifest itself in the back issues of *Bella* or *Better Homes and Gardens*, in fact, properly sifted, our feelings might prompt us towards a career that has nothing at all to do with magazines: We may be more suited to a stationery firm, a psychotherapy practice, or an industrial design studio.

This is partly why we should be careful not to think with ourselves or others about specific jobs and instead focus on qualities within jobs. We should not rush to conclusions like "graphic designer" or "teacher" but rather stick for as long as possible with the pleasures that jobs contain, captured by words such as order, leadership, meaning, calm, team spirit.

At this point we need to invoke the idea of an inner dialogue. As we proceed, one side of the mind must generously, but insistently, question the other. The observer self should ask the everyday feeling self: "So you found this nice. What was it really about the experience that pleased you? It wasn't everything; it was something more specific. Could you go into greater detail?" And the feeling self can say: "I don't know, I'm not sure. It was just sweet." And the observing self can come back: "Give it another go. It's fine that you are unsure; we'll circle around for another approach. Remember, that other time, there was something similar but not exactly the same. What if we compare them?" And gradually the initial hints yield up parts of the information they contain about what really makes us happy or upset—and hence edge us a little way further towards understanding who we can and ideally should be around work.

It isn't only pleasurable sensations that hold out clues for the future. Envy too is a vital, if more unexpected, guide. Shame is a natural response to feelings of envy. However, to feel embarrassed by our envious moments risks encouraging us to repress them—and therefore, to lose out on deriving some hugely important lessons from them. While envy is uncomfortable, squaring up to the emotion is an indispensable requirement for determining a career path; envy is a call to action that should be heeded, containing garbled messages sent by confused but important parts of our personalities about what we should do with the rest of our lives. Without regular envious attacks, we couldn't know what we wanted to be. Instead of trying to repress our envy, we should make every effort to study it. Each person we envy possesses a piece of the jigsaw puzzle depicting our possible future. There is a portrait of a "true self" waiting to be assembled out of the envious hints we receive when we turn the pages of a newspaper or hear updates on the radio about the career moves of old schoolmates. Rather than run from the emotion, we should calmly ask one essential and redemptive question of all those we envy: "What could I learn about here?"

Even when we do attend to our envy, we generally remain extremely poor students of envy's wisdom. We start to envy certain individuals in their entirety, when, if we took a moment to analyze their lives, we would realize that it was only a small part of what they had done that really resonated with us, and that this should guide our own next steps. It might not be the whole of the restaurant entrepreneur's life we want, but just their skill at building up institutions. We might not truly want to be a potter, but we might need in our working lives more of the playfulness apparent in the work of one example we know. What we're in danger of forgetting is that the qualities we admire don't just belong to one specific, attractive life. They can be pursued in lesser, weaker (but still real) doses in countless other places, opening up the possibility of creating more manageable and more realistic versions of the lives we desire.

Exercise

We don't often think of envy as productive. But every envious moment we have offers us a chance to learn about what it is we are drawn to, deep down. By investigating our envy in more detail, we can identify what it is we feel we lack and, with this in mind, reflect on what we should aim for.

Step 1
Think of a person you envy. Make a list of things about them that are admirable.

For instance:
- talks confidently, successful, thinks of her own ideas, wealthy
- listens really well, gets to talk to fascinating people, intelligent, loved by many
- orderly mind, always deliberate, has a secure position
- works hard, takes lots of risks, unafraid of being demanding (around money), ethical.

Now ask yourself what in particular draws you to this person. Is it everything on your list, or do one or two things stand out in making you feel envy and longing?

Step 2

Once you have narrowed down the specific things you envy, ask yourself how you might bring these things into your life. Can you imagine not being this person, but nevertheless having these things you admire (wealth, risk-taking, an orderly mind)? It may be that you have to have them, at least at first, to a lesser degree. But think about what your life would be like with these things added. Then consider the first practical steps you could take to attain them.

We must learn to tease out insights concealed in apparently tiny moments of satisfaction and distress scattered across our lives. Once we see how vague our minds really are—and how naturally tricky it is for us to piece together the answers to complex but highly important questions about our futures—we can gain a new perspective. We start to appreciate that our career analysis is going to take time, that it has many stages, that the reach for an immediate answer can backfire—and that it is a strangely magnificent, delicate, and noble task to work out what one should most justly do with one's brief time on Earth.

Exercise

Sometimes our thoughts about the kind of work we might like to do are very general.

We might come up with things like these:
- I'd like to do something creative
- A bit of travel could be good
- I want to make some money
- It would be great to go into consulting, but I worry it might be boring
- Maybe working for a magazine for a while would be fun
- Politics? Or is that crazy?
- I'm worried about being bossed about
- I'm interested in the civil rights movement
- There's a radio presenter I really like ...

Step 1
Make your own list, no holds barred. Allow yourself to be confused, digressive, and fanciful.

Step 2
Notice but don't be panicked by how vague the list is. We need not be embarrassed by how strange the origins of our career decisions can be. It's totally okay that our first ideas come in fragments and seem scattered and out of focus.

Step 3

Behind each of the items on your list are what we can term points of excitement—experiences that gave rise to these ideas. There may be particular images or scenes that come to mind when you think about each thing. For instance, when you think of going into "politics," you see yourself giving a speech—an image connected to a news story you once saw about Congress.

For each item on your list, identify the key experiences behind it, or the images in your mind. Some points of excitement may sound quite odd: small, even fetishistic. But stick with it.

Examples:
- I went to the Matisse show and saw a movie of him cutting stuff out
- It's so cool what Bill and Melinda did with the mosquito nets in Uganda
- I read about a mansion with a resident chef and thought how great that life would be
- So many kids in my country don't have anyone to look after them
- This documentary on *Vogue*, the people looked so cool: so far from my parents

- I loved being in The Hague and seeing a development of great brick houses
- Traveling around with a glamorous team, car waiting at the airport, advising CEOs.

Step 4

One common mental leap we make is to mislabel our interests. We draw some big conclusions from often very slim foundations.

- You might tell the world that you want a job in consulting, but the truth is that you are excited by the idea of meals being paid for, and having a car waiting to pick you up at the airport. The real interest is mislabeled.

- You say to others, and yourself, that you want a job at a magazine, but your real interest is more specific and idiosyncratic: you are excited by the glamour you happened to see in a documentary about a fashion title, but that actually exists in many more places than just a magazine.

Compare the list you made in Step 3 to the list you made in Step 1. See the conclusions you have drawn from the initial experiences and acts of imagination. Look for any mislabelings.

Step 5

A common omission we make is not to analyze the original excitement or stimulus. We fail to articulate precisely what it is we are interested in.

- You dream of a career as a radio presenter (similar to your hero), but what is the excitement really about? Actually, what you love is conversation and the search for wisdom to live well—which needn't have anything to do with radio.

- You feel that so many kids aren't cared for—you were particularly moved and agitated by a documentary you saw on this. When you probe what this feeling is really about, you realize that you care about people getting the right help to have good relationships—a concern that could be taken up in many fields of work.

Go through your list of underlying experiences and images and describe in more detail what they are really about for you. Why were you moved or excited in this way? Articulate more accurately what you care about in each case.

Conclusion

When we get to know our interests better, one thing that can happen is that our first ideas about what we might like to do start to get revised—and sometimes drop away. Equally, the task of analyzing our experiences and mental images can help us articulate what it is we really want. Clarifying what is motivating can lead us in new and better directions.

2

The Pleasure Points of Work

i. Identifying What You Love

We know that work can in theory be enjoyable, but we're seldom encouraged to isolate and analyze what we can term the distinctive "pleasure points" offered by different jobs. We operate with a general sense that it might be nice to work as (say) a pilot or run a hotel, be a vet or make television shows, yet we are shy to drill into the specifics of where the pleasurable seams within such occupations might lie. We recognize that not even the best jobs can be enjoyable all the time, and that boredom and frustration will mar many a day. However, insofar as any job can engage us sufficiently, it will tend to be because of a few specific sorts of moments of heightened gratification and delight that exist within it—and that are in sync with central aspects of our personalities.

It is uncommon for us to split open jobs in search of these pleasure points or to know our own sensitivities to different examples. We tend to understand quite a lot about what people do, but not so much about what there is, in theory, to enjoy about given occupations. And because of this silence, we can find it hard to gauge where our working tastes might best be met.

We need to start to understand ourselves in terms of the pleasure points to which we are most receptive, and then sift through the labor market according to where given pleasures are likely to lie. However specific a job might be, the underlying pleasure points it yields tend to be capable of being filed under some general categories.

When we stop focusing on the externals of salary or technical prerequisites, we can start to talk of any job as a distinctive constellation of pleasure points.

The task feels tricky because we don't yet have a vocabulary of pleasure. However, if we were to start drawing one up, we could arrive at a list of at least twelve factors that might explain what it is people allude to when they say, in a surface way, that they "love" their job.

No job will have all twelve pleasure points together, or in equal measure. Therefore, a central aspect of knowing our working identity is to determine what our own hierarchy of satisfaction might look like. As we read through a list of pleasure points, we'll realize that certain of these options will speak much more loudly to us than others. We can then start to rank them in order of preference. Our tastes might surprise us. Unexpected themes may emerge, and priorities change along with them. By taking a pulse of our responses to different pleasure points, we'll be granted material with which to start drawing up our own private template of what we need to look for in a job we may one day come to love.

12 Pleasure Points of Work

1. The pleasure of making money

–   You loved the time when you were 9 and made cookies for a stall, sold them to people and turned a profit; it wasn't really the money but the excitement of seeing that people really liked what you'd done and were happy to prove it by giving up something unambiguously valuable. Next time, you added different colored frosting, and it was fascinating to see which colors people went for and which didn't appeal. You learned and it made you confident.

–   You get a thrill out of guessing correctly what other people require—though it's not just guesswork, of course, it's because you're always on the lookout for little revealing signals that people don't even know they are sending. You love profit because it is, in many ways, an achievement of psychology: the reward for correctly guessing the needs of others ahead of the competition.

–   You wander through the world aware of how much could be altered: if you walk along a street, you might think: "That early-20th-century eyesore could be flattened, and a block of beautiful brick buildings put up in its place." You notice a pile of cardboard boxes waiting to be recycled and think, "Isn't there some other use for these?" You grasp that every inefficiency is a business waiting to be born.

–   The special appeal of money for you is the endorsement it brings of your insights and skills; you love how the fact that this year's profits are higher than the year before is a confirmation that you were right in a myriad of little decisions you took over many months. It is the clearest proof of the soundness of your judgment.

– Not everyone sees this, but for you making money is an intellectual pleasure. You like understanding your clients' needs better than they do themselves; you enjoy coming up with a solution to a problem before other people have even realized there is a problem to be solved.

– You like that making money is connected to a set of down-to-earth virtues: understanding, hard work, efficiency, discipline, canniness.

– You know it is nice to have a bit of money (it's pleasant using an express lane at the airport and having the means to buy a work of art at a friend's exhibition), but you are clear in your own mind that this isn't a pleasure of working—it's a pleasure that comes as a consequence of work. What you enjoy about your job is the process of generating a profit by applying your insights to the problems of the world.

2. *The pleasure of beauty*

– You like it when a table is nicely laid: the way an elegant water glass harmonizes with a well-designed knife and fork and a very plain earthenware plate. If a candlestick is placed off-center, you feel compelled to move it to the right position.

–   As a child, you had a watch that you loved because the strap was a compelling color: dark green with small red squares in a line down the middle. You loved carefully wrapping birthday presents for your parents and got bothered when you couldn't fold the ends neatly; you always wanted to use the minimum number of sticky tape pieces (three small strips), not out of a worry that it might run out but because you loved the feeling that the fewest was also the best (although you might not have been able to articulate this at the time). You envied a friend's bike because the wheels were a slightly unusual size, and this seemed to suit their personality. You loved watching boys who were good at playing soccer and you were struck by their different styles: one made lots of rapid, small, nervy movements, keeping the ball close to his feet; another took long, loping strides and had a way of leaning back when taking a big kick.

–   At school you loved carefully underlining the title of an essay: One year you experimented with wavy lines; another time you used a ruler and obsessed about the thickness of the line. Sometimes you spent so long getting the title right you didn't have much time left for actually doing the writing.

- You notice when two buildings are misaligned—it spoils the street, and you wish someone had taken more care and noticed how jarring the conjunction was; you wish you could go back in time and put it right.

- You liked the look in winter of a brown plowed field that led to a line of gray, leafless trees on the horizon.

- You notice and appreciate a nice font on the pages of a book about German history.

- You might enjoy a movie because it has lovely interior shots (you are paying attention to the shape of a room, the placing of furniture, the curve of a door handle); for this, you will forgive improbable convolutions of plot or uninspired dialogue.

- You notice how much more excited you have been than any of your partners when the hotel room is just right.

3. The pleasure of creativity

- You were 7, and all the Lego pieces were on the floor; this was one of the best moments as all the possibilities of the lovely things you might make were there somewhere. You were entranced by the potential. You loved cutting up cardboard boxes (the serrated edge of a bread knife was ideal for the task). There was a memorable time a washing machine arrived in a box so big you wanted to live in it; you made a window flap and stocked it with blankets, pillows, and a bar of milk chocolate. You sometimes wished your favourite songs were a bit different—maybe they should repeat a particularly nice bit, or make their voices go down instead of up at the end; you wanted to fiddle with it (even though it was lovely already). As a child, before you went to sleep at night, you used to imagine other things happening to your favorite characters in a story; how would it have been if they hadn't missed the train—maybe they would have had a whole set of other, even more interesting, adventures? In your sexual fantasies, you're always telling yourself stories about the broader lives of the protagonists: how they dress at work, what the layout of their apartment is, how they felt when they ordered a whip online; sometimes you realize you've even stopped thinking about sex.

–   You love to be asked to imagine and assess the future: should we go into the Japanese market? Is it worth making greetings cards? Should we get involved with the Turkish company? These sorts of thought experiments come easily to you. Sometimes, you like to imagine what the ideal education system or the perfect city might be like.

–	You enjoy considering which images will work best with a presentation and are always trying to come up with better ways of conveying information. One time, you hit upon a photo of a hippo up to its ears in a river to get your colleagues to see the urgency of an issue.

–	People think you like novelty for its own sake, but they couldn't be more wrong; you like better solutions, you just know that they often lie in unexpected places, and you love hunting them down.

4. The pleasure of understanding

–	You used to bother your parents with (in retrospect) slightly nonsensical questions: why are birds called "birds" and not something completely different like "lotheropsicals"? What would baby chimpanzees look like if they were shaved? Do they have time on other planets? You wanted there to be good reasons for things.

–	You were a bit shocked when you realized your father couldn't really explain why plugging in the hairdryer made it work. How could something coming out of the wall force the little fan to turn around?

–   One time when you were 11 a friend said she was jealous of her sister, and you were entranced by the way this idea could make sense of why someone often got angry with someone else.

–   You love to lay down your thoughts on paper. Your mind becomes clearer and your anxiety levels decrease. Some people drink or go jogging to relax. You like to reflect.

–   At school you felt cheated when the math teacher said she couldn't tell you at the moment why this way of tackling a problem actually worked; all you needed to know was that it did.

–   You like it when a news report goes behind the scenes and explains why a compromise was reached, or why a party made a U-turn on its housing policy; it stops being a mystery (you dislike people who like mysteries) and starts to make sense.

–   You often feel people leave things unresolved: they don't explain properly, and they don't seem curious about the multiple possible explanations about why people act as they do.

- You like it when a mass of seemingly conflicting facts can be given a coherent explanation. There's usually an underlying, much simpler and clearer, pattern waiting to be discovered.

5. The pleasure of self-expression

- As a child you liked it when adults asked your opinion (sometimes you got frustrated because you didn't know what your opinion was on this thing, but you really wanted to have one).

- When you were in a school play, you loved the way you could expand on a bit of yourself via a character.

- You get frustrated when people don't listen; you want to make them pay attention.

- Some people think you are narcissistic, but they aren't right: it's that you love sharing things you like with others. It's not self-regard; it's a kind of generosity.

- There was one job you did where a senior manager took you aside after a meeting and told you to pipe down a bit, because what you thought wasn't always relevant to the agenda; later you could see their point, but it really upset you.

– Sometimes you run out of space on feedback forms.

– You love it when people ask good questions about you.

– The idea of writing an autobiography has crossed your mind.

– You'd adore to be interviewed, but often find watching interviews excruciating. You want to shout out: Get to the juice, say the real stuff!

– When you do something, you want it to be obvious to others that you have done it.

– The idea that you could put your personality into making something—a chair, a garden, a government policy—strikes you as strangely alluring.

– You love it when you feel you have "touched someone's soul."

6. *The pleasure of technology*

– When you were little, your aunt gave you a set of screwdrivers arranged in size from micro to jumbo. You hardly ever used them, but you loved the sense that each one was designed to tackle a slightly different situation. There was a lovely moment when there was a problem with a hinge in a kitchen cabinet door and your mother said, "Where's that little set of screwdrivers of yours?" and you found one that fitted exactly (it was a 3mm Phillips head).

– When you were around 6, you stopped taking cars for granted and started to think of them as machines. It was amazing that there were these metal boxes decked out with special dials and little screens and windows that—unlike at home— would open at the touch of a button (or not, if your mother had disabled the back ones). You were intrigued by exhaust pipes and radiator grilles, which hinted at the strange needs of the machine.

– You love the idea that we are still at the beginning of the project of meeting our needs through technology. You like to imagine where we might be by 2180.

– You don't think of technology just as machines and information processing; the pencil appeals to you as a model of technology: simple, intuitive, robust, perfect for its function (you secretly love pencil sharpeners and sometimes sharpen a pencil just for the pleasure of using this perfect little mechanism and seeing a crisp little curl of wood roll off the blade). In your eyes, socks are wearable foot technology.

- You hate it when people associate the future with jetpacks. It will be far more interesting than that.

- You love asking: What's the essence of this problem and how could it be solved more cheaply and easily?

7. The pleasure of helping other people

- As a child, you loved being allowed to join in. Your sister hated being asked to unload the dishwasher, but you rather liked it because you felt you were contributing. You liked the feeling that your mother or father could be getting on with cooking the rice or phoning the plumber because you'd freed them up.

- In make-believe games, you liked rescue scenarios; someone was going to be eaten by piranhas and you'd pull them back onto the raft (which was actually a couch) just in time.

- You liked it when friends told you what was bothering them. You didn't know what you could do, but you liked trying to say comforting things (and sometimes you felt very upset when they rejected your well-intended comments).

- You feel that work is meaningful because it makes a difference to other people; in some way it brings them pleasure or solves a problem they have, and you really like hearing about this. You like the idea of seeing the consequences of what you do in the lives of others.

— Your father used to get frantic when he thought he'd lost the car keys; you liked being the one who could calm him down and say, "Think, what did you do when you came home yesterday evening?" Once he found them in the bathroom.

8. *The pleasure of leading*

— You didn't just want to be in charge, you actually liked being in charge (it was a difference that struck you early). Lots of people at school wanted to be picked as the team captain, but they didn't really like the responsibility, they just wanted the status. What you wanted was the job, the role, the chance to put your ideas into practice.

— You like it when others turn to you for advice. You don't just say whatever comes into your head. You want to solve their problems. You want them to be able to trust your judgment.

— You like it when leadership is earned, not just conferred.

- You enjoy hearing about leaders who haven't succeeded by ordinary standards.

- When you were about 14, you read a story about a general who surrendered to save the lives of his troops; they didn't win, but he was a real leader, you thought.

- When other people get in a panic, you find yourself getting more focused; you like that about yourself.

- When people say they want to avoid responsibility if possible, your first instinct is to dislike them.

- When you were little, you were excited by the idea of fame. It doesn't appeal much now; it just seems like an unfortunate side effect of being good at something.

9. *The pleasure of teaching*

- If someone made a mistake, you wanted to put them right.

- You had a lovely teacher when you were 7; she knew how carefully you were listening and when you were trying (even if you got something wrong).

– You love the feeling of equipping somebody else with your knowledge, of how you can turn their panic and frustration into mastery and confidence.

– You know you have to be careful where you deliver your "lessons"; people don't like to feel patronized, but you like nothing more than filling in the gaps in the knowledge of others.

10. *The pleasure of independence*

– The first time you drove on your own, you never wanted to stop.

– You like getting up very early, before anyone else is around, when you can follow your own projects in peace and quiet.

– For you, growing up has been all about getting away from people who can control you.

– You like being alone; boredom rarely troubles you.

– You recoil from guided tours and tour groups.

– You were extremely excited when you read a story about a guy who quit his job in a bank and started a company importing avocados from Western Africa.

- You really like coming to your own opinion about the merits of a book or a work of art and it doesn't bother you if other people regard you as eccentric.

- You've been accused at times of not being a team player, and there's a degree of truth in the criticism.

- An evening on your own is never a challenge. It gives you a chance to plot and to think. It annoys you how some people always just want to chatter.

11. *The pleasure of order*

- When you were doing homework, you really liked making your writing clear; if you had to rub out a mistake in pencil, you were very careful that the rubbing out wasn't visible. You hated making mistakes in ink and experimented with pasting extra little bits of paper on top of a mistake so as to preserve an overall look of neatness.

- You were fascinated by the cutlery drawer; you loved the fact that each kind of thing had a special place. It bothered you a lot when your sister didn't care and dropped a spoon nonchalantly into the fork section.

- Even if you weren't much good at science, you found the periodic table strangely alluring; you liked the idea of everything being sorted into the constituent elements, with the chaos of the world reduced down to a few elements only. This struck a chord, even if you found yourself looking out the window when the details were explained.

– You hate it when people say "filing" in a sneering way.

– You like arranging sets of coloring pencils according to the color spectrum, although there always seem to be some problems; does yellow shade into white or light green (via greenish-yellow)?

– You get annoyed when people jump around when telling a story ("oh, I forgot to mention …").

12. *The pleasure of nature*

– You can't bear how so many modern windows don't open.

– It was lovely aged 8 to get down on your hands and knees and look closely at a hedgehog or a snail. You felt it could be your friend. You liked imagining its life, which seemed as interesting as any human's.

– You love camping, especially if the weather isn't perfect. It's a more interesting challenge to put up a tent in a storm.

–   You were on a long walk in the country with your family when it started to rain. Everyone complained, but you loved it; you just drew up the hood of your cagoule and liked it when you could feel the raindrops actually splashing on your nose.

–   You had mixed feelings about watching David Attenborough documentaries. You found them very interesting, but you didn't just want to watch them sitting on the couch with a plate of fish fingers on your lap; you wanted to be there, in the swamps of the Serengeti plains during the wet season or clambering over the rocks of the Galápagos Islands; you wouldn't care if you got mud up to your knees or scratched your fingers quite badly.

None of us ever identify equally with all these pleasures. Some stand out and can move up our list of priorities. In the process of reading about them, we may start to discover our personal pleasure-point profile and know that these are the kinds of pleasures we should be looking to develop in our working lives. In talking to others about their work, these are topics we should be probing. If we read about someone's career, we should be on the lookout for what has been pleasurable in their days and tracing where this might intersect with our own pleasure needs. We're in search of the precious zone where our talents and pleasures meet the needs of the world— that is where we should try to locate our future careers.

Exercise

Step 1

Read each pleasure point and see whether it touches on things that excite you or engage with your memories. In the categories that most appeal to you, add details from your own life about things that you've enjoyed in the past or that have given you pleasure in work situations.

It might take a little while for these to come to mind. Once the general idea of noting pleasures is in your mind, you might remember (when waiting to pay at the supermarket or when stopped at a traffic light) something you really liked when you were 10 that belongs somewhere on the list. It can take ages to get to know the contents of our minds, and working out what really gives us pleasure is a lifelong enquiry.

Step 2

Once you've added your own thoughts to a list, some of these pleasures may stand out to you while others may leave you cold. Write down the list of pleasures, with the most important to you at the top and the least important at the bottom.

You will have to make sacrifices in eventually settling on a particular job. Each job will meet some pleasures more and others less: there may be creativity, but less opportunity to lead; or plenty of time spent on understanding, but few opportunities to help others. Ranking the pleasures will give you a statement of what you value most, and thus what you should seek in a job, if necessary, at the expense of other satisfactions.

Step 3

Getting to know our pleasures is a key ingredient in working out what kind of job would fulfill us. But the pleasures on their own don't usually point to a specific line of work. What they do is give us a very good way of examining the suitability of any particular job that one might consider.

Select any job that has crossed your mind at any point as something you might be interested in doing (even if you never took it very seriously). Think of whether this job would offer much scope for the pleasures at the top of your list— the ones that matter most to you.

Even if you come to think that this job doesn't stack up at all well against your pleasure points, this is a valuable gain of knowledge. There's a much clearer sense of why this wouldn't be the right thing for you. Repeat the exercise for all the different jobs you've ever vaguely considered. Flick through the job section at the back of the paper. The goal is to get practice at assessing possible jobs with respect to pleasure points.

Exercise

It's often useful—as a way of jogging our minds and helping us get more into detail—to talk through these pleasures with another person. As we tell them why we liked this, or didn't care so much about that, we tend to find that a lot more information comes to mind, and we get a clearer and deeper sense of our enthusiasms. So a good move now would be to take the ranked list of pleasures and set up a meeting with a friend to go through it and tell them all about it. It's not incidental that this is a good thing to do with a friend. It will also give them a whole lot of new and very interesting insights into you. Ideally, at some point, you'd get to talk through their list too.

ii. The Antifixation Move

One key thing that can go wrong in our thinking about a career is that we get fixated on a particular kind of job that, for one reason or another, turns out not to be a promising or realistic option. It may be that the job is extremely difficult to secure; it may require long years of preparation; or it might be in an industry that has become precarious and therefore denies us good long-term prospects.

Here we call it a fixation (rather than simply an interest) to signal that the focus on the job is problematic because we have an overwhelming sense that our future lies with this one occupation and this occupation alone— while nevertheless facing a major obstacle in turning our idea into a reality.

We might, for instance, get fixated on literary publishing, but find that there are few openings and that the pay cannot possibly cover the rent that would be required to live anywhere within commuting distance of the office. Or we might develop an interest in serious long-form journalism, although its economic base has been substantially eroded. We might become obsessed with the idea of a political career, despite the chances of effecting major change being painfully slim; we might be fixated on a career in movies, although the level of competition is ferocious and the chances of success tiny and horribly unreliable.

The solution to such fixations lies in coming to

understand more closely what we are really interested in. The more accurately and precisely we fathom what we really care about, the more we stand to discover that our interests and their associated pleasure points exist in a far broader range of occupations than we have until now been used to entertaining. It is our lack of understanding of what we are really after—and therefore our relatively standard and obvious reading of the job market—that has pushed us into a far narrower tunnel of options than is warranted.

Fixation doesn't only occur around work. In relationships too, we can become fixated on a particular person whom we love and admire and cannot stop circling—even if, sadly, they happen not to be interested in us or treat us shabbily and unreliably when we are with them. Despite the abuse, we say to ourselves (and to concerned others) that we just cannot imagine an alternative life without them, so special are they (perhaps they are uncommonly funny in certain moods, or play a musical instrument brilliantly, or have a wry pessimism that we adore).

The move to unfixate ourselves is not to tell ourselves that we don't like this person or to attempt to forget how much we are attracted to them. It is to get very serious and specific about what the attraction might be based on—and then to see that the qualities we admire also exist in other people who don't have the problems that are currently making a fulfilling relationship impossible. The careful investigation of what we love about someone shows us—paradoxically but very liberatingly—that we could in fact also love someone else.

Understanding what we like—what gives us pleasure—is therefore a central antifixation move. By strengthening our attachment to qualities, we are weakening our attachment to specific individuals or jobs. When we properly grasp what draws us to one job, we identify qualities that are available in other kinds of employment as well. What we really love isn't this specific job, but a range of qualities we have first located there, normally because this job was the most conspicuous example of a repository of them.

This is where the problem starts: Overly conspicuous jobs tend to attract too much attention, get oversubscribed, and are then in a position to offer only very modest salaries. Yet, in reality, the qualities can't only exist there. They are necessarily generic and will be available under other, less obvious guises—once we know how to look.

Imagine someone who has become heavily invested in the idea of becoming a journalist. The very word "journalist" has become a coveted badge that captures everything they feel they want. From a young age, the job suggested glamour and stimulation, excitement and dynamism. They got used to parents and uncles and aunts referring to them as a future journalist. It started when they were 12. However, the sector now happens to be in terminal decline and is pitiably oversubscribed. A block and angst result.

The recommended move is to pause the fruitless job search and unpaid internships and ask oneself what might truly be appealing in one's intuitive excitement around journalism. What are the pleasures one is really seeking here—and might they exist somewhere else, and somewhere more favorable, in the world of work?

We're prone to a very natural vagueness here. We often just like the broad sound of a given job. But if we pursue the pleasure-point analysis, we start to prise off the lid and look more assiduously at the pleasures on offer. Once we've scrutinized it, we might find that journalism offers some of the following pleasures: an ability to engage with serious political and sociological issues, to analyze policy, to write up thoughts with elegance, and to be respected for one's critical powers.

Once such elements are clarified, it becomes clear that they cannot be uniquely connected to the sector we call journalism. The combination can't only exist—and isn't only needed—in newspapers and magazines. It's not really tied to any particular sector. The qualities can, and do, turn up in a lot of other places. For instance, a financial investment firm might have a huge need to analyze emerging markets and explain their potential and their possible weaknesses to clients; a college might need to analyze and understand changes in its competitive environment and explain these in clear and compelling ways to its staff; an oil company might need to analyze its future likely employment needs and convey this to its recruitment teams around the world. These industries don't sit under the heading of journalism, but they all have needs and opportunities that offer exactly the same pleasures that were initially and rather superficially associated with journalism.

Investigation reveals that the pleasures we are seeking are more mobile than initially supposed. They don't have to be pursued only in the world of the media; they may be more accessible, more secure, and more financially rewarding when pursued in quite different sectors of the economy.

This is not an exercise in getting us to give up on what we really want. The liberating move is to see that what we want exists in places beyond those we had identified.

The same analysis could be run around teaching. This doesn't have to be done in a primary or high school; one might be in essence a teacher in an aeronautics conglomerate (you have to teach new recruits about the nature of the industry) or a wealth-management firm (you have to teach executives how to deal with difficult clients). Or, someone who was fixated on politics might realize that the pleasures they seek (influencing societal outcomes) are as much available (and better rewarded and more consequential) in a job with the tourist board or an oil exploration company.

This can look like a climbdown only if we don't understand well enough what we are actually looking for. The surprising, liberating side of pleasure-point analysis is that it reveals that it can never be a particular industry sector that is the key to finding a job we can love. When properly understood, a pleasure is—thankfully—generic and can turn up in many different and initially unexpected places. Careful knowledge of what we love sets us free to love more widely.

Exercise

Step 1

Our most familiar experiences of moving on from fixations are to be found in the realm of love. Remember a partner you were once fixated with (not a current one), some years ago. What did you like about them? Make a list. Perhaps you liked how they were quiet but spoke intimately with you in person. Or you enjoyed the way they laughed, or their brown hair. Boil down these particular things into general characteristics.

For instance:
- sweetness
- shyness
- humor
- hair.

Now think of times you have been attracted to these same qualities in other people. You know (from having now moved on) that you can find these qualities elsewhere. And this lesson from love can be applied to work: You might be fixated on a particular field of work—but it may not be this specific thing that you should pursue. You can find the same satisfactions and excitements that you seek elsewhere.

Step 2

1.   Write down the job, or jobs, you want to do (but that might be proving tricky to get into): journalism, architecture, politics ...

2.   What bits of the jobs in particular do you imagine being nice? Imagine a day on the job at its best and identify the peak moments.

For example:
-   closing the deal
-   arriving in Hong Kong
-   walking onto the movie set
-   team meeting
-   a site visit.

3. Boil these down to identify the general characteristics of the pleasure:
- negotiating
- travel
- being the center of attention
- taking responsibility
- influencing how places look.

4. Imagine how, around work, these same attractive activities could be pursued. For each underlying theme, make a list of three other places where it could be played out.

Step 3
Normally we apply for jobs in organizations and we have to fit their job description (which lists necessary qualifications, qualities, experience, being a "team player," etc.).

For this exercise, reverse this situation: write your own ideal job advertisement that you believe would best suit who you are, based on your description above of the fundamental things you want to enjoy about work. What would a job that used all your talents and embodied the kind of purposes you feel are important actually look like?

The purpose of the task is to bring together all your thinking about what you love. Think of an advertisement describing the ideal person (you) and the kinds of general things they would do (your ideal)—regardless of whether such a job exists.

For example:
We are looking for a person who:
- loves arranging physical environments
- gets excited by large-scale projects
- loves thinking about relationships and how they can work well
- will take responsibility over a ten-year timeline
- wants to work in an intelligent team.

As part of the job, you will:
- make apps that will be downloaded by millions
- design the way things look
- be involved in purchasing other companies
- have nice dinners, be picked up by a car from the airport, etc.

iii. The Output/Input Confusion

A very common way to identify what job we might like to do is to set our sights on industries that produce the sort of things we enjoy consuming. We enjoy their outputs, and therefore seek to partake professionally in their inputs.

This means that we're pretty likely to write off whole areas of the economy, because they're not obviously connected with offering up things we enjoy consuming. If I'm visually creative, I'm likely to ridicule the idea of working in the cement industry. If I love nature, I'll probably dismiss the energy industry as a bad fit. If I love self-expression, I'm probably not going to see the finance sector as an obvious area to look for a job I could love. We associate sectors with their overt outputs and therefore quickly come to the view that whole fields have little to offer us.

And yet there can be huge benefit in considering jobs not in terms of how we feel about their outputs, but in terms of how our interests align with their inputs. These inputs may not be at all obvious during a first impatient glance, so far are they in tone from the outputs that define the outward character of businesses. So when we think of a given industry, we should ask more rigorously than is usual what must be required to produce its goods and services. What will the people working in it actually be doing so that the obvious output can finally emerge? We don't necessarily need to go on extensive factual missions to find out more; we just need to use our imaginations to make plausible guesses at the many things that must be going on in a business that will have little directly in common with the final output.

From a distance, the shipping industry might sound very far from our interests. After all, we hate the sea and aren't in any way moved by the sight of large container ships docking in ports. But, in terms of inputs, the shipping industry calls on many skills and interests far removed from the obvious output. It involves tasks such as motivating international cooperation around long-term projects and explaining tradeoffs in ways that are realistic and yet bearable to all involved. There will be huge challenges around taking major decisions under conditions of uncertainty; there will be complex legal and political negotiations in the background; it will be necessary to turn masses of data into easily visualized charts showing who is responsible for what; adverts will need to be commissioned and assessed; conferences will need to be organized and catered for; there will be huge needs around internal communication. In other words, there will be many areas of work that are not inherently bound up with sending freight down the Suez Canal. So the fact that one might not be especially interested in shipping—the output—might not be any sign that this sector is the wrong place to be thinking about a possible career.

Or imagine someone who automatically discounts a career in journalism, because they assume (during a first, cursory glance) that it must be focused mainly on writing and analyses of current events. But if we reflect on the matter, we'll start to realize that there must be a huge range of other inputs that accompany the production of the obvious output. Media companies will be heavily concerned about controlling costs, and there will be a great need for careful organization of resources. Learning about the needs and interests of consumers will be a key factor in the success of a media enterprise; developing new business models will be critical, too. So, even if one is not personally interested in producing stories about current events, journalism might still provide many openings for the particular kinds of pleasure one is most interested in: organizing other people, simplifying complex processes, time management, or teaching and learning. These interests don't leap to mind because they aren't part of the output picture of the sector, but they emerge as vital once we start to think more carefully about the required range of inputs.

What holds for the shipping industry or for journalism holds for many other sectors as well. The inputs will often look quite different from the things we initially associate with an industry. Instead of asking whether the output looks like the kind of thing we enjoy, we should be asking whether our pleasures might be included within the input of an industry. It's a modest but hugely liberating move that can usefully expand our sense of where our best opportunities might lie.

Exercise

To think about what goes on behind the scenes in various kinds of work, and therefore what kinds of pleasures are really available, it is useful to look at the inputs and outputs of a range of jobs.

Step 1
Without thinking about it too much, list some jobs, sectors, or industries you find intuitively:
a)   rather appealing
b)   rather unenticing
c)   indifferent—some areas you've just never really thought about.

Step 2
For each type of work:
-   Describe the output: what are the main products and services?
-   Then think of these jobs in terms of the input.
    Try to imagine in as much detail as you can the kinds of work that have to go on in the background for these products and services to be provided.
-   Note how different the output and input descriptions are.

Step 3

Use the list of your pleasures (from the Exercise on p. 70) and compare it with the input-side descriptions. Where might your pleasures join up?

Step 4

Now that you have considered this, revisit the initial (a) pro, (b) contra, and (c) indifferent lists. Is there any movement in your attitudes?

Exercise:

The odd but exciting job

Step 1

Make a list of five jobs you would like to do. Then make a list of fifteen more you would like to do, including your dream jobs, and things that just take your fancy—jobs that sound like they could be nice or interesting. It doesn't matter at all about not being practical.

Step 2

Examine the extended, more imaginative, list of fifteen. What is it about these jobs that attracts you? These might not be careers you would actually pursue—you might have written librarian, stand-up comic, game show host, "someone who works in an orchard," butler, or a role at the United Nations. But these jobs come to mind because they stand for something that excites you.

Probe what part of you the odd-but-exciting-job fantasy taps into. We're not learning about real jobs but learning about our own interests, which (once we've got them on the radar) can show up in more conventional places too.

iv. What Is a Job Like?

As we get a hold on our own pleasure points and build up an idea of who we might ideally be around a job, it brings into view a problem that surrounds our knowledge of different jobs. We often don't actually know enough about what particular careers or work sectors are like to be involved in.

Of course, there's a lot we can find out with a bit of searching: what the pension provisions are; what the canteen serves and at what prices; how much traveling people do; how the performance review system works; whether people go out for drinks after work; what are the promotion prospects; what are average salaries in this sector; which are the up-and-coming firms. All this is very useful to know. But these things don't quite touch on the sorts of issues that the pleasure points bring to the surface. They don't explore the crucially important, yet very rarely asked, question: What is it actually like to do this job or have this kind of career?

What we want to work out is what would it be like to be (for instance) a carpenter, a government minister, a pilot with a new airline, the in-house lawyer of a design brand? We've been exploring what sorts of things we find pleasurable, but these don't on their own point us very clearly to any particular line of work.

The thing we can do is look at work we might be interested in doing and analyze it in terms of the access it could give to the pleasures we've come to see as important to us. How would these kinds of careers measure up against one's own pleasures?

Exercise:
Imaginary interview

We may have read and learned something about what a job is like from job descriptions, blog posts, and talking to others. However, too often we don't focus our thinking around the right areas. We don't process the background knowledge we have in order to make educated guesses about what the work is really like, which will help guide our decisions.

Step 1
Think of a job you are interested in. If you could receive totally honest answers, what questions would you ask a current employee to find out about the real experience of the job?

Your list might include some of the following:
- How do you feel on Monday morning?
- What are the most common anxieties you feel?
- What are the moments in which you feel satisfied?
- What frustrates you about your colleagues?
- What kinds of conversations do you have at work?
- Whom do you admire at work? What is it about them you admire?

- Has your experience of this job changed much over time? In what ways? For better or worse?
- When you are away from work (say on vacation), do you think about your job? What goes through your mind?
- Do you think you are well suited to your job? In what ways (pro and contra)?
- Describe a success at work. Go into detail ...

Step 2

You may never get to ask such questions to an actual employee. But based on what you know about the job, imagine yourself as the employee and make up the detailed answers you would give to each of your questions.

3
Obstacles and Inhibitions

i. Family Work Templates

Even when we eventually arrive at a reliable sense of the kind of career that would ideally suit us, it won't necessarily be the end of our difficulties: we are likely to have to negotiate our way around a variety of psychological obstacles that can powerfully inhibit us from advancing towards the goals we have identified.

One of the most daunting obstacles can be traced back to our families. For most of human history, the working destiny of every new generation was automatically determined by the preceding generation. You would become a farmer or soldier like your father or a seamstress or teacher like your mother. Choices were cruelly restricted, and penalties for deviating from the intended trajectory could be severe. In 18th-century Prussia, the sons of nobles were barred by law from starting businesses or entering trade. In 19th-century England, a respectable father could have his daughter locked up in an asylum if she persisted in a wish to become a singer or an actress. It was conceptually impossible for the child of a lawyer to find employment as a potter or a carpenter.

Then, in the early 20th century, under the sway of a Romantic ideology, societies gradually freed themselves from class and parental strictures. In two central areas—love and work—parents ceded power to their children, leaving choices in the hands of every son and daughter. We were liberated to marry whomever we liked and to do—professionally—whatever we pleased.

Yet these theoretical freedoms have had the curious effect of hiding from us just how much familial expectations continue to matter and to restrict the course of our careers. Our parents may no longer have a legal power to block our bank accounts or physically restrain us, but they retain command over that central tool of psychological manipulation: the threat to withdraw affection in the event that we frustrate their aspirations for us. Love can control us as much as force or the law ever did.

In the background of our minds, there are always what we can term "family work templates" in operation, restricting what sort of jobs we feel able to devote ourselves to and encouraging us towards a set of favored options. Our backgrounds make certain forms of work more or less available.

At the most benign level, our family work templates are the result of what our families understand of the working world. Every family has a range of occupations that it grasps, because someone has practiced them and, in the process, humanized them and brought them within the imaginative range of other family members. There are families where, as long as anyone can remember, there have been doctors around. From a young age, one has heard about the often-comedic habits of patients, the rivalries on the ward, the eccentricities of senior doctors, and the fun and agony of medical school. Hence it is normal and possible to feel that one might, when the time comes, decide to join the ranks of the medical establishment. Other families have generations of lawyers or accountants in them, sailors or hoteliers, blacksmiths or butchers. A child might hear constant anecdotes that stress the fascinations of the courtroom or the impressive character of saving lives; the benefits of education or the vigorous dignity of running a kitchen; the excitement of making a successful deal or the honor of policing the city streets. Exposed to family members in the relaxed settings of home (where the gap between the professional and the personal is at its narrowest and where impressive destinies therefore come to seem very possible), certain jobs naturally end up feeling more plausible than others. Our uncle's career as an air traffic controller won't appear unapproachable when it is practiced by someone we remember mowing the lawn and enjoying jokes with.

Seldom is stepping outside of familial experience presented as plain wrong, wicked, or stupid. But it may just not be something that seems imaginatively available to us. We wouldn't know where to start when no one in the family has ever gone into, say, sport, electronics, or the theater. The people on whose affections we depend can't help us to become confident in such areas. They restrict us not because they are mean, nor because they have carefully studied all the facets of our characters and refuse to accept our true inclinations, but because their own experiences are simply and necessarily rather narrow.

This said, at times, more value-laden dynamics are in operation. The family work template emerges as the result of what parents esteem and aspire to, and, conversely, what they are afraid of and in flight from. In many families, there will be certain career options that the parents speak about with particular reverence: perhaps being a great writer or a senior judge, a principal or a civil servant. These frequently aren't the things that the parents are themselves engaged in; they are what they once wanted to do (but never did).

Many parents quietly hand on their dreams to their children to fulfill—usually without telling them that they have placed these burdens on their shoulders. Yet a message is conveyed that following a given route will be the chief way to secure love and admiration; the son or daughter will be the architect that the parents were too timid to be, or the entrepreneur they were barred from becoming. Nothing like this is ever stated, but the ambitions hover in the psychological ether nevertheless. It doesn't seem like anyone is being strong-armed, but it's remarkable how much we can be influenced by fifteen years of admiring glances cast in particular professional directions—and vice versa.

We're equally liable to receive little messages that certain careers are beneath us and are not quite right for our station in life. Modern parents don't put up absolute barriers. It's not that they'll never speak to us again if we go into asset management or become a sound engineer, but they can create a forceful mental atmosphere in which the negatives of particular kinds of work come across especially clearly. Parents can subtly convey a low regard for jobs that are otherwise perfectly acceptable to society at large; they may quietly give out a sense that no reasonable person could ever wish to work as a dentist, or that accountancy is a profession for the timid; they might imply that being a teacher is a waste of a life or that only unscrupulous individuals could even consider a career in advertising; they may have intimated a view that architects are all slightly deranged or that anything touching on psychology is the realm of charlatans and cranks.

We sense our parents' wishes and excitements and are impressed by them and, because we love them, try to align ourselves with them. It's very natural. But it may be tragically at odds with the kind of work that could actually bring us fulfillment.

In *Middlemarch* (first published in 1871–2), George Eliot tells the story of Fred Vincy, the son of a successful local manufacturer. His parents, whom he loves, strongly believe that he should be a clergyman—not because he is in any way suited for such a job, but because his father thinks highly of such a position, one that he would himself have liked to hold. In the end, Fred becomes a surveyor and is very happy in the job, but George Eliot shows over many pages just what an enormous mental struggle this move has been for Fred. She reveals how painfully conscious he is of letting down his parents; how it creates a rift with his sister, who is embarrassed by his work; and how he senses that his friends from college think he's a failure. George Eliot tells us a story of someone who almost doesn't manage to liberate himself from a parental template, because she is well aware that many of us never manage to make the break that Fred achieves. This shouldn't surprise us: In a choice between love and our own satisfaction, it is understandable if we often close down our horizons so as to preserve our relationship with those who brought us into the world.

What distinguishes modern societies from their predecessors is how quietly the messages about what it is wise to do are emitted. Fred Vincy's parents may talk to him directly about his career choices and bully him in concrete terms. But few parents now operate in this way. Yet this is not the same as giving a child true freedom to do whatever he or she thinks is right. Because the family work template is only ever implicit, we don't necessarily see what a powerful effect it may be having on us. In order to free ourselves, we have to actively make ourselves consider the net of family expectations we are likely to be enmeshed in.

We should ask ourselves what lies within the circle of familial work experience and what outside of it—and consider whether certain legitimate options have been discounted for arbitrary or snobbish reasons. We should ask ourselves what unfulfilled dreams our parents had for themselves and whether these may be resting on our shoulders in ways that don't align with our deeper selves. We should wonder how our parents privately ranked careers. Even if they overtly said—of course—that all jobs can be good ("we just want you to be happy"), we need to grasp the particular way in which they did imply that some jobs were more worthy than others.

Then, through such patient explorations, we will start to see what influences might still be lingering, foreclosing certain important options and perhaps holding us back from wholeheartedly embracing a career that we suspect, in our heart of hearts, really is right for us.

Exercise:
Familiar and unfamiliar

Step 1
Make a list of the jobs or kinds of work that were familiar to you, as things done by family members and people you knew well. What were the jobs that felt obvious— as the kind of thing someone from your family would naturally do?

Step 2
Now consider the kinds of work that were outside the collective range of your family's experience (growing up, you might never have spent time with an accountant, a rural doctor, a TV presenter, a math teacher, an HR specialist, or someone who worked for a major pharmaceutical firm). List some jobs that felt completely outside the family norm, but that might be surprisingly appealing to you.

Exercise:

Good and bad

Our inherited family template around work includes ideas about what makes a job good or bad, admirable or a bit suspect. Families have value systems even if they aren't explicit about them; it is useful to focus on what yours might have been in relation to work.

Step 1

Did you ever get the impression that your parents regarded some kinds of work in a negative light (they might not have agreed on this)? For instance, they might have had a far from positive view of lawyers or of school teachers; they might have implied, even if they never said it outright, that any form of manual labor is only for other people, or that someone who doesn't do something vaguely creative is to be pitied. Make a rough list of some jobs your family would have considered "bad." What did they think was actually wrong with them? What's your own view? Do any of the bad jobs appeal to you—or might they appeal, if you could set aside the views you've heard?

Step 2

Make another list of the jobs your family held in high regard. What did they think was right or good about them? How do you really see these lines of work? What might actually be not very satisfying or attractive about such careers?

Exercise:

Anecdotes

Step 1

Think back to ways your parents mentioned the struggles and successes of their work—perhaps in anecdotes at dinner, or in what they would say when they came home exhausted some days. Make a list of everything you remember your parents said or thought about work—their own work, other kinds of work, and working in general.

For instance:

- Clients always want the cheapest thing and don't understand the vision.
- Big companies ruin things.
- Small firms always get eaten by big ones.
- Teaching is a dead end.
- You have to develop a whole life plan before you even get a job.
- No one ever knows what they should do; we all just wing it and hope for the best.
- There are lots of people who get away with being rubbish at what they do.
- Merit is the key to all success.
- Colleagues are often lazy, selfish, and stupid.
- It's great working with people who are a bit better at something than you; that's how you learn.

- It's no good doing anything unless you get to the very top.
- The bosses are always just in it for themselves.

Step 2

If a private investigator was asked to investigate you and the paths you have taken or dreamed about, could they find clues about how these background assumptions and opinions have played out in your life? Are there particular elements you have reacted against? Are there opinions and views you have endorsed as prominent parts of your own worldview? Which elements of your own outlook have come from your own exploration and reasoning, and which elements have been passed on to you from the imaginative environment created by your family?

ii. Fixing Parents

One of the most important, but necessarily rather secret, indicators that we are on the right track with our work is a sense that we are doing better than our parents. Far from this suggesting meanness or cruelty on our part, it can be a legitimate sign that we have alighted on an occupation that feels meaningful and invigorating for us.

But we need to focus on what "doing better" really means. Traditionally, the term has been interpreted financially. A generation is understood to be doing better than the last when it can live in bigger houses and afford fancier vacations.

Yet there is a more interesting and more subtle way of interpreting the notion of "doing better." The term can also be applied to situations where we are able to correct some of the psychological compromises, blind spots, or excesses of our parents through our work. There will most likely always be something missing from the life experience of those who brought us up. Perhaps Dad wasn't having enough fun. Perhaps he was scarred by financial instability when he was little and that's why he judged work primarily in terms of security. Perhaps Mom was a bit frantic in her search for adventure—in reaction to her own excessively stultifying upbringing. She loved artists who hadn't quite made it yet and radical moviemakers who never would. She was brilliant at mimicking her conventional brother, who was the butt of a lot of family jokes.

A career choice is at some level often semi-consciously guided by a desire to heal aspects of our parents' psyches. One might be trying to demonstrate, for instance, that it is possible to care about stability and have a personally meaningful career, or that one can be a person with a soul and also be interested in worldly success. One may want to show that one can manage to do well in finance and at the same time be close to one's children, or to be thoughtful and interested in science. We are vitally spurred on by attempts to go beyond certain of the limitations of our progenitors.

Our eventual career choice can be seen as an attempt to compensate for some of the drawbacks and confusions of our parent's lives—without breaking faith with everything that was important to them. We can be driven by a transgenerational project of healing and correction. We like to think that we can work out everything in the span of our own lives. But it may really take the combined experience of two or three generations to piece together a wise and effective (and satisfying) attitude to work. No doubt some of what we haven't achieved will be left to our own children to take up.

Therefore, a revealing question to ask is: How might we want to exceed our parents psychologically—at the level of maturity and happiness—through our work? What would it mean to put right the errors of thinking and feeling of the previous generation? How could we help our parents (even if they are dead or not especially interested in our assistance; the unconscious doesn't tend to factor in such details)? These questions can help us to focus on our own developmental needs.

It is useful and instructive to want to exceed our parents—not to humiliate them, but to correct certain flawed attitudes from which they have suffered. Perhaps our parents were (through no particular fault of their own) unstrategic or too provincial; naïve or excessively cynical. They have lived out their particular problems, but we don't have to. We can digest their setbacks and be educated by them. In choosing a career, we should take time to ask ourselves at the outset what it would really mean for us to do "better"—in the deep sense—than our parents.

Exercise

One of the less obvious but important ways a job can be right for us is that it allows us to improve on our parents' experiences of work. Here's an exercise to target what that might mean for you.

Step 1

Think back to the ways your parents were annoyed or frustrated by the work they did. What would they say was missing in their careers? And what, in your view, were the deficiencies and excesses of their working lives?

Was their working life:

- too unexciting
- too risky
- exhausting or demoralizing
- unambitious
- too focused on pleasing others
- too bound up with relentless targets?

Step 2

For each problem, ask yourself what sort of job you would need to do in order not to have that problem in your life. It might not be a "better" career (by the standard measures) than your parents had. For instance, it might not necessarily pay more or have more social status. Why, to you, would it feel like an improvement on your parents' experience of work?

iii. The Dangers of Success

We might imagine that, in an uncomplicated way, our parents (and siblings, friends, and wider families) will always be pleased at our successes. After all, they were delighted when we scored highly in a spelling test at the age of 6, so there is no apparent reason why they wouldn't always be happy about our triumphs, however large or varied they might be.

But this risks missing out on a crucial, rather secret, piece of human psychology: how unsettled our successes can make other people around us, especially our parents. Consequently, we might unconsciously want to spare them worry, or we might opt to defy their feelings, but at the cost of considerable anxiety and guilt on our part (a dynamic that might lead to moments of career self-sabotage).

It is natural for parents to seek closeness with their children; they invest enormous amounts of time inducting them into their worldview and educating them to be competent and adept. But that love does not come without conditions; it is almost always hemmed in by covert pacts and demands. At a certain point, parental generosity runs up against boundaries determined by an older generation's potentially fragile self-esteem and sense of achievement. There may come a point at which children threaten to undermine their parents, not through sloth and indolence, but its opposite: through vigorous achievement that separates them from the home they came from and quietly indicts the parents for how they have led their lives.

The successes of children can throw into relief the multiple and usually unspoken regrets and compromises of mothers and fathers, especially if these successes coincide with signs of retrenchment in parental careers: perhaps a father has been moved sideways and it is clear won't now ever get to head office; perhaps the mother is having to go down to three days a week to look after her own ailing mother.

At such moments, we may feel a guilty inhibition about pursuing our ambitions at full throttle. Our fear isn't so much that we might fail as what the consequences might be if we managed to succeed. Rivaling a parent (or indeed a sibling) can be a thrilling covert project—but at the same time, a frightening one we might choose to retire from early.

Success, though longed for, is not an uncomplicated state. It attracts admiration, but also envy. It emphasizes our virtues, but, unwittingly, delivers a humiliating verdict on the status of those around us. We tend to locate the reasons for career setbacks in the external world: in the frustrations of office hierarchies and the vagaries of the economy. But sometimes the reasons are purely internal ones, nothing to do with a lack of skill on our part, but rather a psychological inhibition about overtaking those who have nurtured us. We can "fail" in order to keep succeeding at other things we're attached to, like not humiliating our parents.

When interrogating ourselves about the progress of our careers, we might dare to ask ourselves some strange but useful questions: Who might be upset if I succeed? Over whom might I have a covert desire to triumph? On whom am I seeking revenge? We might also try ending some sentences:

– *If I succeed, my father might feel ...*
– *If I succeed, my mother would feel ...*

There is, of course, an alternative to success: self-sabotage. We should recognize how unnerving satisfaction can feel. Although happiness is what we believe we seek, it often isn't really what we know. We may have grown up with, and learned to make our peace with, far darker scenarios. The prospect of a satisfying career, when it appears, can therefore seem counter-intuitive, and not a little frightening. It isn't what we've come to expect, and it doesn't feel like home. We may prefer to choose what's comfortingly familiar, even if it's difficult, over what is alienatingly fulfilling or good. Getting what we want can feel unbearably risky. It puts us at the mercy of fate; we open ourselves up to hope—and the subsequent possibility of loss. Self-sabotage may leave us sad, but at least safely, blessedly, in control. It can be useful to keep the concept of self-sabotage in mind when interpreting our odder antics around careers. We should start to get suspicious when we catch ourselves pulling off poor performances around people we need to impress. We may be trying to stay loyal to an unhappy version of ourselves.

We should be careful too around "friends." The word goes in inverted commas because of how many of these so-called friends don't exactly follow the rules of friendship as we like to tell ourselves they exist. Groups of friends are frequently silently held together by shared fears and vulnerabilities. What the friends are all afraid of is as important as what they all admire. The success or new initiative of one friend can therefore undermine the delicate psychological economy of the group. On the surface, our friends may say that anything we do is fine by them, but in reality, certain choices can radically undermine their own life choices. If we are leaving medical research to go into business, how wise have they been to insist that they had no interest in money? What would it say about our friends' last decade in publishing or accountancy if we promptly decided to join a tech company or a cattle ranch?

We should be generous towards the envy of others: it comes from a weak, fragile place. Yet it means we may not always find encouragement and support in places we might expect it—not because we are in the wrong, but because our rightness unnerves others. We may be made to feel we are in error, but we should have the sangfroid and psychological distance to imagine that this could be self-serving talk and that every career move has the potential to bring us into conflict with those closest to us. The price of doing what we want may be to upset people we love. We may have to drop some friends, make others and recalibrate our relationships with family. Knowing that these are all necessary and normal parts of succeeding can give us the courage to deal with one of the most difficult features of moving ahead with our careers.

Exercise

We don't normally go around thinking that success carries dangers. But this fear may be lurking, unsuspected but potent, at the back of our minds and obstructing us from making our best efforts. This is an exercise to help locate such anxieties.

Step 1

In what ways might your success upset your parents, even if they would not overtly tell you, and even if they concurrently felt pride in your success?

For example, they might feel one of the following:

- They didn't really make the most of opportunities themselves.
- If they told you the truth about their working lives, you would feel sorry for them, which they would hate.
- You might no longer be impressed by their achievements, which would seem trivial beside your own.
- They'd find it hard to cope if you had more money than them (for instance, a father might like to be the

one who always pays for everything; even if it's made out to be a burden, it's a heroic burden, and that would be taken away).

Step 2

In what ways might your success upset some of your friends? Imagine rising quickly to a position of considerable responsibility, or making a small fortune, or getting a chance to spend time around well-known people. Can you imagine this secretly making some of your friends envious, or fearful that you might stop being interested in them?

Step 3

Which of your friends or colleagues wouldn't be so supportive if you announced a change in jobs? Why do you think this would be? They might, for instance, feel that you were indirectly reproaching them for not being more adventurous. They might take it to imply that a job that's good enough for them isn't good enough for you. They might worry that you would change personally, in a way that would threaten the friendship.

Step 4

How are your friends and family invested in you continuing with what you're doing now? It could be things such as: they've grown used to you doing this; they helped you get started and it would feel a bit ungrateful to change; they like being able to pigeonhole you via your job. They worry that all change involves risk and don't want to see you get hurt.

iv. Confidence and Inner Voices

We don't often dwell on this—and may never discuss it with others—but when it comes to responding to the challenges we face around our careers, many of us have voices in our heads. We have a murmuring stream of thoughts inside our minds that constantly comment on our aspirations and achievements.

Sometimes, the voices are warm and encouraging, urging us to find more strength or to give an initiative another go: "You're nearly there, stick with it"; "Don't let them get to you; rest and you'll be ready for a new fight tomorrow." Yet sometimes, the voices are harsher and more condemnatory; their tone is defeatist and punitive, panic-ridden and humiliating. They don't represent anything like our best insights or most mature capacities. These aren't the voices of our better nature. "Stupid fool, imagining you knew a way to beat the odds." "You've always run away from the real truth about yourself ..."

Speaking to ourselves in these stern ways may feel natural, but another person in a similar situation might have a very different kind of inner monologue in their head—and they might reach their goals a great deal more effectively as a result. Being successful is, after all, to a critical degree a matter of confidence: a faith that there is no reason why success would not be ours. It's humbling to recognize just how many great achievements have been the result not of superior talent or technical knowhow, but merely of that strange buoyancy of the soul we call confidence. And this sense of confidence is ultimately nothing more than an internalized version of the confidence that other people once had in us.

An inner voice is always an outer voice that we have previously heard, absorbed, and made our own. Without our quite noticing, we have internalized the voices of the many people who have dealt with us since infancy. We may have assimilated the loving, forgiving tone of a grandmother, the unruffled perspective of a father, the humorous stoicism of a mother. But along the way, we may also have absorbed the tone of a harassed or angry parent; the menacing threats of an elder sibling keen to put us down; the words of a schoolyard bully, or a teacher who seemed impossible to please. And we have absorbed such unhelpful voices because at certain key moments in the past they sounded extremely compelling and unavoidable. The messages were so much a part of our world that they got lodged in our own way of thinking.

Part of mastering a career we can love involves coming to terms with our inner voices. We need to tease out what voices characteristically operate in our minds, what they are telling us, and where they are likely to have come from. We need to audit the voices and edit out some of the less helpful ones. For this, it helps to remind ourselves that we have a choice about the voices we entertain. We should strive to ensure that the way in which we speak to ourselves becomes more conscious, less the result of accident, and that we have planned for the tone we will use henceforth in response to the challenges we're confronted with.

Improving the way we speak to ourselves means encountering and imagining equally convincing and confident, but also helpful and constructive, alternative inner voices. These might be the voices of a friend, a therapist, or a certain kind of author. We need to hear such voices often enough and around tricky enough issues that they come to feel like natural responses—so that, eventually, they come to feel like things we are saying to ourselves; they become our own thoughts.

The best sort of inner voice speaks to us in a gentle, kind, and unhurried way. It should feel as if a sympathetic arm were being put around our shoulder by someone who had lived long and seen many difficult things but was not embittered or panicked by them. This speaker would be someone who took their time, worked their way through setbacks, and eventually either succeeded or could accept failure without self-hatred.

In certain states of humiliation around work, in many of us, there is a feeling that our difficulties rightly debar us from love. We need to incorporate a voice that separates achievement from sympathy: that reminds us that we may be worthy of affection even when we fail, and that being a winner is only one part—and not necessarily the most important part—of one's identity.

This is, traditionally, the voice of the mother, but it might also be the voice of a lover, a poet we like, or a 9-year-old child chatting to their mom or dad about stress at the office. It is the voice of a person who loves you for being you, outside of achievement.

Many of us grew up around nervous people: people who lost their tempers the moment the parking ticket couldn't be found and who were knocked off course by relatively minor administrative hurdles such as the electricity bill. These people had no faith in themselves and therefore—without necessarily wanting to do us harm—couldn't have much faith in our own abilities. Every time we faced a test, they got more alarmed than we did. They asked multiple times if we had enough to wear when we went outside. They worried about our friends and our teachers. They were sure the vacation was going to turn into a disaster.

Now these voices have become our own and they cloud our capacity to take an accurate measure of what we are capable of. We have internalized voices of irrational fear and fragility. At certain moments, we need an alternative voice that can pause our runaway fears and remind us of the strengths we have latent within us, which the currents of panic have hidden from us. Our heads are large, cavernous spaces; they contain the voices of all the people we have ever known. We should learn to mute the unhelpful ones and focus on the voices we really need to guide us through the difficulties of our careers.

Exercise

The aim of this exercise is to take an audit of our own inner voices.

Step 1
Ask yourself what you characteristically say when you:
- fear something bad will happen
- assess how things have been going
- are annoyed at someone
- find a task tricky
- realize someone is late
- have to do something you don't want to do
- achieve something.

Doing this shines a spotlight on how we speak to ourselves, although this is familiar in a way we don't often notice. And it gets us into the habit of observing how our own minds work.

Step 2
How would you characterize the things you say to yourself? Which are negative and which are positive and helpful?

Step 3

Can you relate any of these inner voices to people from your past? Which ones? Try to pin a person or persons to each identifiable voice.

Step 4

Find the kindest one: imagine if it spoke more loudly and more often. What would it say to you on which occasions?

v. The Perfectionism Trap

We typically aim for a particular career because we have been deeply impressed by the exploits of the most accomplished practitioners in the field. We formulate our ambitions by admiring the beautiful structures of the architect tasked with designing the city's new airport, or by following the intrepid trades of the wealthiest Wall Street fund manager, by reading the analyses of the acclaimed literary novelist or sampling the piquant meals in the restaurant of a prize-winning chef. We form our career plans on the basis of perfection.

Then, inspired by the masters, we take our own first steps, and trouble begins. What we have managed to design, or make in our first month of trading, or write in an early short story, or cook for the family is markedly and absurdly beneath the standard that first sparked our ambitions. We who are so aware of excellence end up the least able to tolerate mediocrity—which, in this case, happens to be our own.

We become stuck in an uncomfortable paradox: Our ambitions have been ignited by greatness, but everything we know of ourselves points to congenital ineptitude. We have fallen into what we can term the "perfectionism trap," defined as a powerful attraction to perfection shorn of any mature or sufficient understanding of what is required to attain it.

This isn't primarily our fault. Without in any way revealing this, or even perhaps being aware of it, our media edits out billions of unremarkable lives and years of failure, rejection, and frustration even in those who do achieve—in order to serve up a daily curated selection of peak career moments, which thereby end up seeming not like the violent exceptions they are, but a norm and baseline of achievement. It starts to appear as though "everyone" is successful because all those who we happen to hear about really are successes—and we have forgotten to imagine the oceans of tears and despair that necessarily surround them.

Our perspective is unbalanced because we know our own struggles so well from the inside, and yet are exposed to apparently pain-free narratives of achievement on the outside. We cannot forgive ourselves the horrors of our early drafts—largely because we have not seen the early drafts of those we admire.

We need a saner picture of how many difficulties lie behind everything we would wish to emulate. We should not look, for example, at the masterpieces of art in a museum. We should go to the studio and there see the anguish, wrecked early versions, and water marks on the paper where the artist broke down and wept. We should focus on how long it took the architect before they received their first proper commission (they were over 50), dig out the early stories of the writer who now wins prizes, and examine more closely how many failures the entrepreneur had to endure.

We need to recognize the legitimate and necessary role of failure, allow ourselves to do things quite imperfectly for a very long time—as a price we cannot avoid paying for an opportunity one day, in many decades, to do something that others will consider a spontaneous success.

Exercise

Perfectionism is a form of impatience and a misunderstanding of how right things need to be in order to be viable.

Step 1
Consider someone you deeply admire operating in your field. List their greatest achievements.

Step 2
Identify or try to imagine their failures; you might not know details, but picture projects that didn't work, schemes that failed, books that weren't so good, movies that bombed, deals that soured.

Step 3
Draw a life line of your hero's work trajectory: How much time was spent in compromise or failure? How much was able to go wrong and yet things were still, broadly, on track?

Step 4

Perfectionism involves the idea that failure is incompatible with success. It develops, in part, from exaggerated anxieties about what would happen if things didn't go well.

- How do you define failure? Do other people usually define it like this?
- When have you failed?
- What have the consequences been? Were they as bad as you anticipated?

vi. The Duty Trap

We start off in life being very interested in pleasure and fun. In our earliest years, we do little but hunt out situations that will amuse us, pursuing our hedonistic goals with the help of puddles, crayons, balls, teddies, computers, and bits and pieces we find in the kitchen drawers. As soon as anything gets frustrating or boring, we simply give up and go in search of new sources of enjoyment—and no one appears to mind very much.

Then, all of a sudden, at the age of 5 or 6, we are introduced to a terrifying new reality: the "rule of duty." This states that there are some things, indeed many things, that we must do, not because we like them or see the point of them, but because other people (very intimidating, authoritative people who may be almost three times our size) expect us to do them—in order, so the big people sternly explain, that we'll be able to earn money, buy a house, and go on vacation about thirty years from now. It sounds pretty important—sort of.

Even when we're home and start crying and telling our parents that we just don't want to do the essay about volcanoes for tomorrow, they may take the side of duty. They may speak to us with anger and impatience—beneath which there is simply a lot of fear—about never surviving in the adult world if we develop into the sort of people who lack the will to complete even a simple homework assignment about lava and want to build a tree house instead.

Questions of what we actually enjoy doing, what gives us pleasure, still occasionally matter in childhood, but only a bit. They become matters increasingly set aside from the day-to-day world of study, reserved for vacations and weekends. A basic distinction takes hold: pleasure is for hobbies; pain is for work.

It's no wonder that by the time we finish college, this dichotomy is so entrenched, we usually can't conceive of asking ourselves too vigorously what we might in our hearts want to do with our lives: what it might be fun to do with the years that remain. It's not the way we've learned to think. The rule of duty has been the governing ideology for 80 percent of our time on Earth—and it's become our second nature. We are convinced that a good job is meant to be substantially dull, irksome, and annoying. Why else would someone pay us to do it?

The dutiful way of thinking has such high prestige because it sounds like a road to safety in a competitive and alarmingly expensive world. But the rule of duty is actually no guarantee of true security. Once we've finished our education, it emerges as a sheer liability masquerading as a virtue. Duty grows positively dangerous. The reasons are twofold.

First, because success in the modern economy will generally only go to those who can bring extraordinary dedication and imagination to their labors—and this is only possible when one is, to a large extent, having fun (a state quite incompatible with being exhausted and grumpy most of the time). Only when we are intrinsically motivated are we capable of generating the very high levels of energy and brainpower necessary to shine out amid the competition. Work turned out merely out of duty quickly shows up as limp and lacking next to that done out of love.

The second thing that happens when our work is informed by our own sense of pleasure is that we become more insightful about the pleasures of others—that is, of the clients and customers a business relies upon. We can best please our audiences when we have mobilized our own feelings of enjoyment.

In other words, pleasure isn't the opposite of work: it's a key ingredient of successful work.

Yet we have to recognize that asking ourselves what we might really want to do—without any immediate or primary consideration for money or reputation—goes against our every educationally embedded assumption about what could keep us safe, and is therefore rather scary. It takes immense insight and maturity to stick with the truth: that we will best serve others, and make our greatest contribution to society, when we bring the most imaginative and most authentically personal sides of our nature into our work. Duty can guarantee us a basic income, but only sincere, pleasure-led work can generate sizeable success.

When people are suffering under the rule of duty, it can be helpful to take a morbid turn and ask them to imagine what they might think of their lives from the vantage point of their deathbeds. The thought of death may usefully detach us from prevailing fears of what others think. The prospect of the end reminds us of an imperative higher still than a duty to society: a duty to ourselves, to our talents, to our interests, and our passions. The deathbed point of view can spur us to perceive the hidden recklessness and danger within the sensible dutiful path.

Exercise

Step 1

When you were growing up, did you think about work as something you were supposed to enjoy? Try to remember specific occasions: perhaps you were 10 and coming home from school and it struck you that you'd have to get a job one day. Did you imagine this to be exciting, like an adventure, or more like a chore, like always having to do something you didn't really want to do? Why do you think you had the attitude you did?

Step 2

If you were guaranteed an adequate income but had to do something (anything) for at least forty hours a week, what would it be? Do you feel more enthusiastic about hobbies and leisure pursuits than about work? How would you feel differently if you took away feelings of duty?

Step 3

If duty were not an issue, what would you do?

vii. Impostor Syndrome

In many challenges, both personal and professional, we are held back by the crippling thought that people like us could not possibly triumph given what we know of ourselves: how reliably stupid, anxious, gauche, crude, vulgar, and dull we really are. We leave the possibility of success to others, because we don't seem to ourselves to be anything like the sort of people we see lauded around us. Faced with responsibility or prestige, we quickly become convinced that we are simply impostors, like an actor in the role of a pilot, wearing the uniform and making sunny cabin announcements while incapable of even starting the engines. It can feel easier simply not to try.

The root cause of impostor syndrome is a hugely unhelpful picture of what other people are really like. We feel like impostors not because we are uniquely flawed, but because we fail to imagine how deeply flawed everyone else must also be beneath a more-or-less polished surface.

Impostor syndrome has its roots far back in childhood, specifically in the powerful sense children have that their parents are very different from them. To a 4-year-old, it is incomprehensible that their mother was once their age and unable to drive a car, tell the plumber what to do, decide other people's bedtimes, and go on planes with colleagues. The gulf in status appears absolute and unbridgeable. The child's passionate loves—bouncing on the couch, Pingu, Toblerone—have nothing to do with those of adults, who like to sit at a table talking for hours (when they could be rushing about outside) and drinking beer that tastes like rusty metal. We start out in life with a very strong impression that other people—especially competent and admirable other people—are really not like us at all.

This childhood experience dovetails with a basic feature of the human condition. We know ourselves from the inside, but others only from the outside. We're constantly aware of all our anxieties, doubts, and idiocies from within. Yet all we know of others is what they happen to do and tell us—a far narrower and more edited source of information. We are very often left to conclude that we must be at the more freakish and revolting end of human nature, but we're far from it. We're just failing to imagine that others are every bit as disturbed as we are. Without knowing exactly what it is that troubles or racks another outwardly very impressive person, we can be sure that it will be something. We might not know exactly what they regret, but there will be agonizing feelings of some kind. We won't be able to say exactly what kind of unusual sexual kink obsesses them, but there will be one. And we can know this because vulnerabilities and compulsions cannot be curses that have just descended upon us uniquely; they are universal features of the human mental equipment.

The solution to impostor syndrome lies in making a crucial leap of faith—the leap that others' minds work in basically the same ways as ours do. Everyone must be as anxious, uncertain, and wayward as we are. It's a leap of faith because we just have to accept that the majority of what we feel and are, especially the more shameful, unmentionable sides, will have a corollary in each and every one of us.

One of the tasks that works of art should ideally accomplish is to take us more reliably into the minds of people we are intimidated by and show us the more average, muddled, and fretful experiences they have. That way, we would be helped to understand that we are not barred by our vulnerabilities from doing what they do. This is what the philosopher Montaigne (1533–1592) was attempting to do when he playfully informed his readers in plain French that "kings and philosophers shit and so do ladies."

Montaigne's point is that for all the evidence that exists about this shitting, we might not guess that these people ever had to squat on a toilet. We never see distinguished types doing this—while, of course, we are immensely well informed about our own digestive activities. And therefore, we build up a sense that because we have crude and sometimes rather desperate bowels, we can't be philosophers, kings, or ladies; and that if we set ourselves up in these roles, we'd just be impostors.

It's a neat example because, despite the lack of evidence, we know that these exalted people must of course excrete in exactly the same way we do. With Montaigne's guidance, we are invited to take on a saner sense of what grand, powerful people are really like. But the real target isn't just an under-confidence about bodily functions; it extends into the psychological arena too. Montaigne might also have said that kings, philosophers, and ladies are racked by self-doubt and feelings of inadequacy, sometimes bump into doors and have weird lustful thoughts about members of their own families. Furthermore, instead of considering only the big figures of 16th-century France, we could update the example and refer to CEOs, corporate lawyers, news presenters, and successful startup entrepreneurs. They too can't cope, feel they might buckle under pressure, and look back on certain decisions with shame and regret. No less than shitting, such feelings are not what separate us from them. Our inner frailties don't cut us off from doing what they do. If we were in their roles, we'd not be impostors; we'd simply be normal.

Making a leap of faith around what other people are really like helps us to humanize the world. It means that whenever we encounter a stranger, we're not really encountering a stranger, we're encountering someone who is, in spite of surface evidence to the contrary, fundamentally very much like us—and that therefore nothing fundamental stands between us and the possibility of responsibility, success, and fulfillment.

Exercise

Step 1

Think about vulnerabilities you have that other people wouldn't necessarily know or expect you to have. Even though you think your vulnerabilities are obvious, there remain lots that you are good at hiding. Imagine someone being surprised to discover certain things about you. What would they be surprised by?

Step 2

Ask yourself why these failings and vulnerabilities of yours are not always obvious to others. Do you conceal them out of nastiness, out of a desire to deceive and trick others? Or are there other, less sinister, reasons? Perhaps you are not trying to hide them at all. If your failings quite often stay hidden, there's a very good chance this will happen with other people too.

Step 3

Now imagine the exercise the other way around. Think of a person you admire and try to imagine them not letting on about their troubles—for simple, unthreatening, undisturbing reasons. What might their flaws and fears be?

viii. The Job Investment Trap

Quite often the prospect of moving to a job you can love looks very difficult because it involves a period of humiliating retrenchment. There's going to be, at least for a while, a drop in salary; you are going to have to acquire new skills; you might have to move back home; there's going to be a period of relative incompetence; others your age will be much further ahead in this particular line of work; you'll be condemning yourself to perhaps a few years of low status. It can feel humiliating and slow. It goes against the grain for ambitious people, who have a strong natural drive to get going immediately, to see quick, tangible results, and to make obvious progress. The idea of further training can feel deeply off-putting. The job investment trap looms when another career looks very alluring in principle but the investment in time and dignity required to get there feels so negative that you push the whole idea aside and give up—to your great eventual cost.

Ironically, the job investment trap is at its most potent when we are young. Imagine someone who is 20; they'd been planning a career in chemical engineering and they're well on the way to gaining the right qualifications. They selected particular subjects at school, took the right courses at college, did some relevant work experience, got to know a few people who were already in the kinds of jobs they'd had an eye on. They've already made a big investment. But now they start to think very seriously that they should be looking at an entirely different kind of career. Maybe in order to find a job they can love, they should be looking at becoming a landscape architect or a marine biologist. It's probably going to mean a job investment of at least two years.

At 22, two years feels like a very long time indeed. It's 10 percent of the whole of one's life so far. Psychologically, it's even bigger than that. At 20 you've maybe only felt you were "you" since you were about 16—before that, you were in the daze of childhood and adolescence and didn't have any real idea of what your life might be about. So two years feels like half your existence. It's a vast commitment.

What's so hard to grasp—and yet essential—is how things will look in the future, aged say 56. From there, two years has a very different meaning. It's only 1/20th (or 5 percent) of the 40 years between being 16 (and starting to take a real interest in the possibilities of work) and being at the climax of middle age. Over time, the length of further study grows relatively small against the backdrop of a whole working life, while the consequences of not having undertaken it grow ever larger.

A similar thing happens around what we might call the "love investment trap." You've maybe been with someone for a couple of years and although things are sometimes quite nice, you sense that overall it's not really a very good relationship. But you stick with it because the investment required to find a more suitable partner is daunting. The present looms too large and the long, long future—which will in fact constitute by far the greater part of our lives—doesn't carry the weight it really should.

There are two big reasons for this. One is that the long future is linked to a narrative of decline. The idea of getting older isn't something we embrace and feel excited about. We're squeamish about ageing. We don't usually look forward to being 56 or 67, and so we find it easy, even appealing, to avoid thinking about what our interests and needs will be at these future stages of existence.

We live in a culture that is very impressed by youth. We're constantly reminded of why it's nice to be young and rarely encouraged to dwell on what might be appealing or interesting about getting older. So we don't imaginatively invest in working out what will help us live well in middle age. To counter this tendency, we should draw up timelines to force ourselves to see that the period from 16 to 24 is quite short in comparison with that between 24 and 48 or 48 and 72. In the cultural utopia, when we were 22, we'd frequently watch movies and read books about the lives of the middle-aged. We'd regularly remind ourselves that people's mid-50s are typically the high point of their working lives—the period when they accomplish and earn the most. We'd be doing this to build up our imaginative engagement with our own future existence, so that we'd weigh up investments now not against our most recent experiences but in the light of a more accurate picture of the shape of a whole life.

The other key factor that makes it fatally easy to discount the long term is that we typically live in time zone bubbles. We spend most of our lives around groups of people who are roughly a similar age to ourselves, so we don't get enough intergenerational experience. We don't get drawn into the inner world and experience of people considerably older than we are, and so don't get the full sense of the reality of their stage of life.

We need to have a more active strategy. We have to push people to try to explain their life experience to us. We have to ask leading questions; we have to probe and follow up. We have to ask them to go into more detail. We need to ask specifically how their outlook has changed across the years, what they've come to see differently and why. And we should do this not just with one individual, but in a general and regular way. It can seem strange, but on reflection it is actually reasonable and practical, to think that in order to make our way towards a job we can love, one of the things we might need to do is spend time developing relationships with people quite a bit older than we are. They do not necessarily have to be people involved in careers we're actively considering. The point is more general. We're in search of assistance in taking very seriously something that is crucially important, and yet amazingly easy to discount: the reality of our own future decades of life.

We're in search of ways to help ourselves think more fully and realistically about the future so we can take major decisions in a more clear-eyed way. It's maybe only then that we can properly evaluate the worth of a difficult but important investment that will—at a cost that might come to look worthwhile—help us find a career we can really believe in.

Exercise

If you knew you were going to live to 200 (retiring at around 173), how would you view spending two years retraining for another career? Would it change your thinking? Often it's interesting to imagine that one is short of time, as it is a good way of focusing on priorities. But it is also useful to take the opposite view. What if there were no urgency? You could give scope to parts of your personality that usually get edged out. You might not worry about getting a "proper" job so soon because there would be decades to get round to it later. You wouldn't worry about retraining or switching careers because the future would be so long it would be worth it. This is a thought experiment that helps us see what's on our minds but is normally suppressed because of anxieties about time.

Exercise

Step 1

Think back to conversations you've had with people you know well, who are twenty or thirty years older than you, apart from your parents and extended family. Our thinking about future stages of our own lives is hugely shaped by the experiences we've had (or may have lacked) of a close-up view of people's lives at stages far removed from our own.

Step 2

Leaving aside the negatives for a moment, what might be nice about being 45 or 60 or 75? We live in a culture that tends to be very admiring of youth. That can make getting older feel solely like a disaster, which curiously makes it harder for us to think seriously about our own long-term flourishing. But if we can at least sometimes think it might be rather nice to be older, we get a better perspective: We can care more readily about our long-term future and perhaps be less anxious too.

Step 3

What regrets or worries can you anticipate having when you hit those numbers?

ix. If It Were a Good Idea, I Wouldn't Be the One to Have It

Sometimes our ideas about the kind of work we really want don't tally with anything that exists at the moment. We come up with a picture of a job or enterprise we could love but when we look around the world, we don't see it anywhere. We realize that if we're to proceed, we will have to invent our own solution; we'll have to become an entrepreneur. There's a lot of excitement in our societies about entrepreneurs; they can seem to embody the summit of achievement. But there are also a host of fears about what might be required to start off on one's own. It's easy to get discouraged and to doubt the soundness of one's original impulses.

Often, at the center of our self-doubts, the fact that something doesn't currently exist seems in our minds to indicate that it can't be worthwhile. What's happening isn't really that we've discovered that our idea is no good. Rather we are finding it difficult to imagine ourselves as the locus of originality. We have insights and ideas, but we discount them, because we have had them. We're dealing here with a particular kind of low self-confidence that saps away at our faith that we could be the originators of something important.

The very word "entrepreneur" is a slightly unfortunate designation. It can hint that there's a special kind of person, perhaps uniquely shaped from birth, who has a rare aptitude that we cannot reasonably expect to possess ourselves. They are entrepreneurs; we are not. We build up a mental portrait of such people as radically different from ourselves, in possession of some magical, incomprehensible—though admirable—quality of soul. To get round this obstacle, we need to rethink just what it is that entrepreneurs do.

Our initial associations might lie in terms of someone who makes lots of fundraising presentations, who stays up late at night drinking coffee and poring over spreadsheets, who is very interested in technology and who lives in a loft and rides a special kind of bicycle. But these are all incidentals. In essence, a creative entrepreneur is someone in command of an accurate thesis about what others truly want.

It might initially seem as if it shouldn't be too hard to learn of the wants of our fellow humans. All we would need to do is to go and ask them. The products and services of the future should be determined by gathering a random sample of people and asking them what they would like to buy one day. But a peculiar and rather stubborn problem rears its head at this juncture: Other people don't usually know ahead of time what they want, need, or like. Even if they may one day respond enthusiastically to a given product, they cannot give its creators the information they need to bring it into being. They can confirm, but not originate, ideas. The vast majority of the great innovations could not have been arrived at from the results of a poll or focus group.

The creative entrepreneur is therefore forced

to fall back on a trickier and more unexpected data source, one that is easily overlooked because it is so ubiquitous, lacking in prestige and (this is perhaps the main reason) desperately hard to make sense of: our own minds. When we are attuned to them, our minds and bodies are infinitely sensitive instruments that, minute by minute, yield extraordinary clues as to our needs and satisfactions and, by extension, because human nature has a lot of commonality within it, the needs and satisfactions of others as well. Proper introspection, an ability to read ourselves accurately, with imagination and clarity, without sentimentality or prejudice, provides us with almost everything we might need to know about the key requirements of those around us—upon which sound businesses can be built. Knowing ourselves and understanding other people are, in terms of innovation, often essentially the same thing.

Successful introspection of a kind that leads to innovation involves a good deal of bravery because of how much of what we sincerely like, want, or are opposed to differs from what society defines as normal. Prevailing assumptions about procedures and products often contain ideas and stock responses that have drifted far from underlying truths, but that everyone is too polite, inhibited and disconnected from their authentic responses to question. Staying loyal to ourselves may mean having to be disloyal to rather a lot of what is prestigious.

The successful innovators, be they in art or business, are those who can remain true to insights that would have seemed, when first made, to be very close to bizarre. Edward Hopper (1882–1967) could not have been the first person to feel the lonely charm of the railway station or the strangely comforting anonymity of the late-night diner or the eeriness of Sunday in the suburbs. But those who came before him had too swiftly abandoned their sensations because these had no support from society at large. The figure we call the artist or entrepreneur is, among other accomplishments, someone who minds far less than others about being thought somewhat weird as they go about rescuing and building upon some of their lesser-known yet profoundly significant sensations. Hopper became a great artist through an acute loyalty to his own perceptions.

For most of the history of modern architecture, the elevator has been one of the least loved and most "repressed" of architectural elements. Lift shafts have been elaborately hidden away, deemed to be inherently uninteresting and not worthy of our gaze. And yet occasionally, particularly when we were children, some of us will have had the feeling of being very interested in the hidden bits of lifts, in moments when the doors opened and we caught a glimpse down the shaft itself and observed a fascinating echo, an array of cables, pulleys and balancing mechanisms far outstripping in interest anything we might have seen in the rest of the building. The British architect Richard Rogers became a great innovator (and entrepreneur) in part because he knew how to be loyal to these feelings of excitement around technology in general and lifts in particular. Rather than doing the polite and obvious thing, he stayed true to his enthusiasm, remaining confident that many of us might share it beneath our surface impassivity. Beginning with the Pompidou Centre (1971), his buildings have always left their lift shafts exposed, thereby making our journeys between floors moments in which to admire technical ingenuity and feel our spirits rise in contact with the dynamism and intelligence of modern engineering.

John Montagu (better known as the Earl of Sandwich) had access to all the best options for lunch in his era (1718–1792). He could have had a steak served on a silver platter, or some grilled chicken wings with roast beetroots; he might have been offered an onion pie or a bowl of white soup. But he was acute enough to realize that, while he was playing cards with friends in his central London club, he would ideally like something that would enable him to eat with one hand at relative speed and without the danger of getting his fingers greasy. Therefore, he called for some meat to be held between two pieces of bread. Rather than acting on a mere eccentric whim (as it might have appeared to a startled waiter), Sandwich was identifying an unnoticed, but brilliantly precise, answer to a need that had never been attended to.

It doesn't seem a coincidence that Sandwich was an aristocrat. Even though his most famous invention is now daily fare for millions of ordinary office workers, it bears the stamp of a mind with the confidence to take its own data seriously, a mind without a hint of inner obeisance or feudalism.

Long before they are social categories, feudalism and aristocracy are, in a sense, categories of mind. The feudal mind, which can exist in any class, imagines that others will invariably know better, and that the task is to obey. The aristocratic mind, which you don't need to be an earl to have, allows that, despite all those who have come before, it might still be in charge of a major discovery. Sandwich had the confidence to follow a key thought experiment of the innovator: He could ask himself what he would want to do or think if he could be confident enough of withstanding the laughter and criticism of others.

In 1841, the American philosopher Ralph Waldo Emerson published his most profound essay, "Self-Reliance." In it, he set himself the task of trying to understand where greatness comes from, in business, government, science, and the arts—and his answer was touchingly close to home. Geniuses are those who know how to introspect and trust in their own sensations and ideas: "To believe your own thought, to believe that what is true for you in your private heart is true for all men, — that is genius," wrote Emerson. Although the temptation is always to believe that others must have the answer, the innovator "learns to detect and watch that gleam of light which flashes across his mind from within, more than the lustre of the firmament of bards and sages ... In every work of genius we recognize our own rejected thoughts:

they come back to us with a certain alienated majesty."

The difference between the creative and the uncreative mind isn't, therefore, that the creative person has different thoughts, but that the creative person takes what is in their mind more seriously. What enables them to do this is a quality very dear to Emerson: a capacity to resist the fear of humiliation.

Mediocrity is the result of being guided more by what other people typically do and say than by the thoughts and feelings that are circulating (just below the surface) in our own minds. We know inside, in a muddled way, what could be done, but don't trust our quiet intuitions. We in effect abide by a submissive, feudal story: that it is only other people who have permission to originate good ideas.

Now that the cereal bar exists, it possesses an aura of inevitability. But it was 1975 before it emerged, the work of the inventor Stanley Mason (also responsible for the squeezable ketchup bottle). The root of the problem was a now-familiar fear of oddity: the fear of seeming absurd in creating a product constituted merely from a few dry, congealed cereal flakes. For decades, people had had the experience of returning home, putting a hand in the breakfast carton and eating flakes without milk, but they did not take their maneuver seriously. They failed to acknowledge that they were having an experience that, if commercialized, could found an industry. The fear of being strange continues to quash a sizeable share of our best ideas.

The point of examining these instances of entrepreneurship is to shift the internal blocks around our own ideas about the kind of work we really want to do. The fact that an idea hasn't yet been carried out doesn't mean that it isn't a good idea. What makes it a good idea is really the precision and clarity with which it latches onto our own sense of what we like and enjoy. That's a reason why making such a careful analysis of one's pleasure points isn't an indulgent or marginal undertaking: it's the high road to understanding what it is we might have to offer other people.

Exercise

Step 1
Go through a day noticing and recording the things that please or bother you.

These might be apparently trivial:
- I really liked the way the bus driver stopped and started smoothly; maybe they take pride in their driving.
- I couldn't hold a takeaway coffee, an umbrella, and a briefcase all at the same time.

Or more substantial:
- It was impressive the way the junior partner brought the discussion back into focus and summed up the issue very simply and clearly.

- I felt awful all morning because I kept thinking about the silly row I had with my partner yesterday evening, but I couldn't bring myself to apologise because it wasn't really all my fault.

Step 2

What might be invented out of your dissatisfactions, longings, and loves? Where do these frustrations and pleasures point in terms of products and services? Not everything will lead to a viable, concrete conclusion (there may be no real market for special clips for attaching a paper cup to the shaft of an umbrella). The aim of asking yourself this is rather to get into the habit of taking your own reactions (positive and negative) seriously as hints about the needs of others.

Exercise:

Fixing a piece of the world

Step 1

What part of the world that is broken most pains you? What hurts you to hear about, what touches you, what makes you cry, what captivates you when you watch television? Is it that parents and children stop speaking, that war happens, that children are orphaned, that buildings are ugly, that education is slow and uneven?

Step 2

The next step is to see what you, individually, can do about that problem. The task is to look at what skills you might have that can help. Are you a good negotiator? Do you know what it's like to grieve? Could you design cheaper apartments that retain aesthetic ambitions?

Step 3

Finally, look at the intersection of the big world problem and what you can contribute to it. Locate the small bit of overlap where you have something distinctive to offer in order to help repair the world.

x. Evolution Not Revolution

When we're thinking of making a shift in career, we can easily get dismayed by the scale of the change we're contemplating. We imagine change in dramatic, volcanic terms. We feel we're looking at a revolution in our lives. Everything will have to be different. And that's often going to be a very daunting and unwelcome prospect.

We should recognize that our picture of what change might look like and how it might take place can become a problematic, inhibiting factor. We may stick with what is familiar or take the opposite tack and suddenly and dramatically plunge into a massive revision, resigning and taking off on a journey to another continent. We search for things that are unknown to us; we look to the extremes. That's because we're guided by the natural (but mistaken) notion that if change is going to occur at all, it's going to have to look dramatic.

This fateful habit of mind crops up around relationships as well. Things are difficult and we know we need to make some move to improve our lives. But instead of engineering a series of smallish changes that could help our current relationship to go a bit better, we take the volcanic option: We have an affair, move out, or get divorced.

A more helpful approach is to think in terms of smaller steps and gradual alterations: that is, in terms of evolution rather than revolution.

Evolution is a deeply valid process of change, but

it is a tricky idea for us to have faith in. One reason we don't latch onto it is that it's very hard to see it in action—and hence to believe in its existence. When evolution is at work, there is rarely a decisive moment when change looks obvious. It's like children growing up: We don't usually observe any alteration day by day, yet over time an 11-month-old infant crawling on the carpet and deeply excited by a plastic orange keyring becomes a six-foot-tall 17-year-old obsessed with mountain biking. We know that a million small changes have been occurring every single day in the intervening years, but they almost never announced themselves as major steps. In the background, bones were growing, ligaments expanding, neural pathways being formed, skills gradually accumulating, attitudes and interests taking shape.

It's partly to help us get a better perspective on personal evolution that we've made such a big collective commitment to birthdays. They provide regular moments of comparison that are sufficiently far apart that we can recognize the cumulative effects of little changes. That is why it's moving to mark a growing child's height on the kitchen door. Week by week, no change is observable to the human eye. But the marks edge upwards every year. It's an artifice that compensates for a natural frailty: the difficulty we have around believing in processes we can't see.

Our brains are just not very good at tracking evolutions.

It's also an issue that historians have long wrestled with. If you want to account for the huge changes in a society across a hundred years, it's tempting to look mainly at the biggest public events (the election of a new government, the death of a major public figure, a war, a peace treaty). But in reality, it's often the accumulation of millions of tiny developments that has really made the difference. It's less exciting to read about, but it's more accurate in terms of explaining what has actually been going on and why things have ended up as they have.

So it's not surprising that we find it hard to take an evolutionary approach to our own lives. We're not sufficiently practiced at seeing the relationship between small steps and large overall alterations. But in order to find a job we can love, we would be wise to try out some modest first moves. It may start with taking a single evening class every week, or spending three days during the vacations exploring an option, or retraining part-time in a process that might be finished in two years. An enormous shift might be set in motion by nothing more outwardly dramatic than volunteering for a new responsibility in one's existing job. Minor moves can strengthen our courage by giving us a sense of a talent in an area where we as yet have very little experience. They break through the unhelpful but widely prevalent sense that we should either remain as we are or change everything. Oddly, there is a far less glamorous, more neglected third option that we must explore: the careful evolutionary step.

Exercise

Rather than putting pressure on ourselves to plan and execute a major move, we might try out branching projects or small adventures on the side. What small changes can you make that would help you to see if you have talents in an area, without making the big, revolutionary step of committing to it?

For instance:
- Ask to try out a different area of work within your organization.
- Take a vacation, not to a place but to a job; ask to follow someone around for a week of observation.
- Become good friends with someone who has this kind of job already.
- If you'd have to change where you live, spend time visiting the kind of place you'd move to.
- If the people who do this job tend to go to particular bars or pubs, go there yourself.
- Imagine you are an actor preparing for a role playing someone in this job. Read what they read, buy what they buy; imagine yourself in character.
- Do an internship below your pay grade.
- Do an evening course.

xi. The Energizing Force of Death

A standard piece of decoration in the studies of important people in the early modern period was a skull. This stark reminder of the brevity of life was not meant to leave owners depressed by the vanity of all things. Rather, it was meant to embolden them to find fault with specific aspects of their experience, while at the same time to grant them license to attend more seriously to others. The thought of death has an unparalleled power to shake us from our ordinary "immortal" lethargy and to prompt us to focus our minds on what we might truly want to do.

We spend far too long imagining that there will always be time to sort out our real ambitions later on. It can be useful to panic ourselves while there is still time. In *A Confession* (1882), a record of the fruitful panic unleashed in him by the thought of death, Leo Tolstoy explained how, at the age of 51, with *War and Peace* and *Anna Karenina* behind him, world-famous and rich, he had recognized how, from an early age, he had lived not according to his own values, or to those of God, but to those of "society." This had inspired in him a restless desire to be stronger than others; to be more famous, more important and richer than they. In his social circle, "ambition, love of power, covetousness, lasciviousness, pride, anger and revenge were all respected." But now, with death in mind, he doubted the validity of his previous ambitions. "'Well, you will have 6,000 desyatinas of land in Samara Government and 300 horses, and what then? ... Very well; you will be more famous than Gogol or Pushkin or Shakespeare or Molière, or than all the writers in the world – and what of it?' I could find no reply at all."

The answer that eventually quelled his questions was God. He would spend the remainder of his days living in obedience to the teachings of Jesus Christ. Whatever we make of the particularly Christian solution to Tolstoy's crisis of meaning, his skeptical journey follows a familiar trajectory. It is an example of how the thought of death may serve as a guide to a truer, more significant way of life; it is a solemn call to determine our priorities.

Herodotus reports that it was the custom towards the end of Egyptian feasts, when revelers were at their most exuberant, for servants to enter banqueting halls and pass between the tables carrying skeletons on stretchers. The effect of the thought of death is perhaps to usher us towards whatever happens to matter most to us, be this drinking beside the banks of the Nile, writing a book, or making a fortune. At the same time, it might encourage us to pay less attention to the verdicts of others, who will not, after all, have to do the dying for us. The prospect of our own extinction may draw us towards the way of life we value in our hearts. It may not be cruel; it may indeed be the kindest thing to integrate a powerful awareness of death into our search for work we can love.

Exercise

Step 1
Calculate how many more years you may have to live in relation to an average life span in your part of the world. Frighten yourself by cutting off twenty years for cancer or a heart attack (the two great killers). The point is to create some useful, constructive anxiety about the limited time one has left—to combat the tendency to suppose that there's not much urgency about getting round to the things that one feels are important in one's life.

Step 2
If you had only one year left, what would you do? If you want to take a twelve-month vacation, what does this say about your idea of work? Could you imagine that if you had one year, you'd want to spend a lot of it working? What would your job need to be like to make you feel that way?

Exercise

What do you want people to say of you at your funeral? They'll say a lot of nice and moving things, of course, but focus here on the things that you would count as true achievements—especially things people might not think of mentioning (or even know about) unless you briefed them carefully.

For instance:
- How you conquered your anxiety around starting out on your own.
- How you learned to cope better with authority.
- How you learned to feel that life is not always happening elsewhere.
- How you found a way to integrate your creative side with your job (which didn't seem at first as if it would give any scope for that).

4

Consolations

i. Happiness and Expectations

The big aim across this book has been to understand the project of being happy at work. As we have seen, central parts of this aim are connected with discovering more about one's own ambitions and character and matching this to an appreciation of the needs of the working world. But in any consideration of the concept of happiness, we must take another element into consideration: the issue of expectations. How happy we can be in any context depends crucially on how happy we expect to be. Our happiness is dependent not simply on how good things are, but on how they stack up in comparison with what we imagined could plausibly happen.

Our modern attitudes to career sit on top of a long, complicated history. We're not normally aware of this, but our expectations around work, earning, and status are far from "natural" or eternal. They are the outcome of a complex web of ideas concerning mobility and the chances of success that developed over centuries.

In the Middle Ages in England, if you lived in Bristol (which was then a busy but small seaport), you probably wouldn't know much about what was happening in London, Paris, or the royal courts of Spain. Nonurgent information would simply never circulate around the country: for example, news that the ladies at court liked to gather their hair up in net bags on either side of their faces or that they liked red gauntlets sewn with pearls in floral patterns.

Blanche of Lancaster, first wife of John of Gaunt and mother of Henry IV, was the best-dressed woman in mid-14th-century England. But she couldn't be *fashionable*—because it just took too long for people to find out about what she was wearing.

The daughter of a well-to-do merchant in Bristol might take a great deal of interest in clothes, but she couldn't compare herself with the grander ladies of London such as Blanche—because she simply didn't know what they were up to. In any case, Blanche hardly seemed to belong to the same species.

Then, in August 1770, the first edition of *The Lady's Magazine* appeared.

Every month, it carried detailed illustrations of what the most prestigious women were wearing, so news about bonnets and high waists could circulate rapidly around the kingdom. It also reported on the social activities of the wealthy and esteemed in a tone that felt at once chatty and intimate, as though these grandees were really our friends.

Thanks to the tone of the stories, Lady Bedford was no longer an abstract, unknown aristocrat as remote as a species from another planet. She was someone a few years younger than you, with a very pretty waist, blue-gray eyes, and a delicate fan from Venice, who had recently been to a party at the home of the Marquess of Dorchester, where they served herring pie and shoulder of mutton with thyme and the carriages were due after 1 a.m.

The *Lady's Magazine* started circulating fashion news
to the provinces in the 1770s.

Anyone reading could at last compare their own clothes and social engagements with those of the rich and well connected in London. And so they were provided with the opportunity to experience a rather novel emotion: the feeling of having been wretchedly left out by fashion, society, and the world. They could sit by the window in the small village of Finchingfield in Essex, watching dull gray clouds scudding across the horizon, and know for the first time that life truly was elsewhere. Up until then, you might have been left out, of course,

Illustration from *The Lady's Magazine*, 1812.
Knowledge of fashionable upper-class life increased dissatisfaction
with ordinary circumstances.

but only by people you knew and who lived around you. Perhaps your cousins didn't take you blackberry picking, or the vicar didn't ask you to dinner. The magazine, however, presented itself as a reliable agent for revealing where every lady in the land was spending time and what they were wearing—except you.

In truth, *The Lady's Magazine* was not the disembodied voice of the spirit of the age speaking with universal authority. It was a precarious publication concocted by a man called John Coote in an unprepossessing office in Watling Street, near St Paul's in London. But magazines can have a habit of sounding as if they are the source of ultimate truth when you flick through them in a disconsolate mood in an armchair in your parents' house in rural England.

The new media of the 18th century set about teaching a broad cross-section of society about the incompleteness of their lives: a yeoman farmer could learn from *The Spectator* that he was a clodhopper; *The Tatler* encouraged local squires to recognize their conversation as provincial; *The London Magazine* reminded the merchants of York that they were spending their lives in the wrong city; and teenage girls understood from *Town and Country Magazine* that any prospective husband would be lacking a great many attributes compared to the paragons it had identified. More efficient printing techniques, the use of special-colored inks, a reliable road system, and cheaper postage had conspired to open up new and unfamiliar possibilities for self-disgust.

We don't envy everyone who has more than we do. We envy those we have been taught to compare ourselves with—and with whom we feel in certain ways equal. In the old world, it would not have occurred to any ordinary person to envy an aristocrat or monarch. These exalted characters lived in separate realms and went to great lengths to show the rest of the world how different they were—and how inconceivable it was that one could ever get to be like them. Their clothes, habits, and ways of life made it clear one should never assume they were normal in any way.

Louis XIV of France (1638–1715) liked to wander about in ermine cloaks and gold brocade coats. He carried a golden stick. He sometimes donned a suit of armor. It was extremely haughty and unfair, of course. But it did have one great advantage. You could not possibly believe that you, in all your profane ordinariness, would ever reach the summit. You couldn't possibly envy the mighty, because envy only begins with the theoretical possibility that one might be rightfully owed what the envied person already has.

The modern world is, by contrast, founded on an apparently generous sense that everyone is, in fact, owed the same things. Not in terms of current possessions and status, but in terms of potential. There is no limit to what any of us could achieve. Today, you may be a little short of cash, low on prestige and bruised by rejection. But these are—so it's insinuated—transient troubles. Hard work, a positive attitude, and bright ideas have every chance of

Hyacinthe Rigaud, *Portrait of Louis XIV*
(1638–1715), 1701.

breaking the deadlocks in due course. It's all a question of willpower. There are always encouraging stories in circulation of those who have put in the effort: for example, the person who trailed around South America for five years not doing very much of anything, then came back home, straightened out his life, and founded a business now worth more than many of the world's poorer countries. To reinforce the sense of equality, he doesn't have a suit of armor; he looks as though he could be a math teacher or the taxi driver who picked you up at the airport. Modernity never ceases to emphasize that success could, somehow, one day be ours.

Yet there is unwitting, exhausting cruelty in this narrative of ongoing potential and of merit eventually finding its reward. The data is clear that only a very few of us will succeed. Society is still a pyramid, and the top remains very narrow. The dreams invested in us, by our families and our earlier selves, will almost by definition not come true. And yet despite all the evidence, we find it agonizingly hard to accept that frustrated lives are the norm.

If this were not bad enough, it is especially frightening to contemplate failure in conditions where one is held responsible for it. The old world looked at failure as an accident, as falling into the realm of bad luck or created by the unknowable machinations of the gods. Those at the poorest level of society were known as "unfortunates"— etymologically, people not blessed by the Goddess of Fortune, a deity who handed out her favors without intelligence or design. No merit or disgrace could be attached to one's position in the world. But in the modern world, failure moves from looking like an accident, and therefore the natural target of the charity and sympathy of the wealthy, to seeming like a direct consequence of a personal failing. In a meritocratic age that believes that winners make their own luck, the unfortunates start to be called a far less kindly name: losers. We are held to be the sole authors of our biographies, and therefore, able to take all the credit—and the blame—for the outcome. No wonder that suicide rates rise exponentially in the modern era. To the discomfort of poverty is added the stinging psychological burden of shame.

The old world had been kind with its pessimism. It was everywhere made apparent that life was fundamentally, rather than incidentally, frustrating and that the wisest approach was to learn to practice, from an early age, a philosophy of resignation and renunciation. However skillfully one wielded the scythe or with whatever diligence one raked the fields, it was clear that one would never fundamentally change one's lot. As Seneca (4 BCE–65 CE), one of the best-known and loved writers of the premodern West, understood: "What need is there to weep over parts of life? The whole of it calls for tears." Or as Nicholas Chamfort (1741–1794), that embittered and impoverished French writer of genius, put it: "A man should swallow a toad every morning to be sure of not meeting with anything more revolting in the day ahead."

The pessimists were being sweet. They were attempting to free us from the burden of expectation. They could see that a vast unthinking cruelty lay discreetly coiled within the magnanimous assurance that everyone could discover satisfaction on this Earth. They understood that when an exception is misrepresented as a rule, our individual misfortunes, instead of seeming to us quasi-inevitable aspects of life, will weigh down on us like particular curses. In denying the natural place reserved for longing and disaster in the human lot, the modern world's ideology of hope has denied us the possibility of collective consolation for our fractious relationships, our stillborn ambitions, and our disappointed careers, and condemns us instead to solitary feelings of persecution for having failed to meet expectations that were perhaps not so natural to begin with.

Ideally, the human imagination would be limited to prompting ambitions that were within practical reach. We would not be such inveterate dreamers. But our hopes inherently overshoot. They don't pause for an accurate assessment of both our personal abilities and how hospitable the outer world might be to our plans. We have been endowed by nature with hope-breeding capacities that are beneficial to the species, but may not work to our own particular advantage as individuals. As with salmon leaping up waterfalls to return to their original spawning grounds, we are hardwired with imperatives (to succeed, to win, to master), which have no regard for our personal ability to deliver on them. Nature doesn't care that we ourselves can't write a particular sonata or launch a cherished business idea; our drives are independent of our talents to deliver on them. Only one salmon in a thousand ends up reproducing successfully ...

The optimism of the modern world has vastly increased opportunities for happiness, but also hugely expanded the specter of panic and foiled perfectionism. It has moved a great many areas of human activity from the realm of things that were deemed very likely to go badly wrong to the realm of things that could and should be perfect. It has made the ideal the norm and internalized the burdens of failure.

Modernity has placed an infinity of choices before us, but forgotten the tragic fundamental that we never understand enough about ourselves or the world to make reliably correct choices. We lack the relevant information and experience, yet have to make decisions that will have huge implications for our own lives, and the lives of others. Should we expand into the South Korean market? Is this the time for a large-scale rebranding exercise? Do I resign if I don't get this promotion? Should I take the job in New York, or take up the offer in Tangiers? If my partner's career takes them to Germany, do I follow, or do we break up over this? If there are children, do I take on more work (to pay for things) or less work (to spend more time around them)? Should I try to get into the property market now, or wait for the correction?

By the time we have reached middle age, we will have made several hundred big decisions. Of those, fifteen might have been very, very wrong and we will be paying for the errors for the rest of our lives. This is the dilemma at the heart of Existentialism—a philosophy developed in Denmark in the 19th century, which drew compassionate and intelligent attention to the difficulties created for humans by having insufficient knowledge and time to make optimal choices. The great Existentialist Søren Kierkegaard (1813–1855) wrestled all his life with the issue of whom he should marry. For a time, he thought he'd found the answer: an attractive young woman called Regine Olsen. Regine rejected him at first, then accepted him, at which point he began to have doubts. The saga took up a good decade and caused enormous damage on all sides. The pain led Kierkegaard to one of the most beautifully intemperate passages in his masterpiece *Either/Or*—as applicable to marriage as to any other area of choice:

> Marry, and you will regret it; don't marry, you will also regret it; marry or don't marry, you will regret it either way. Laugh at the world's foolishness, you will regret it; weep over it, you will regret that too; laugh at the world's foolishness or weep over it, you will regret both. Believe a woman, you will regret it; believe her not, you will also regret it ... Hang yourself, you will regret it; do not hang yourself, and you will regret that too; hang yourself or don't hang yourself, you'll regret it either way; whether you hang yourself or do not hang yourself, you will

regret both. This, gentlemen, is the essence of all philosophy.

The Existentialists offer us a useful corrective to the normal, pernicious view that intelligent choice might be possible and untragic in structure. A Kierkegaardian approach tempers the modern sentimental notion that perfection is within reach. That you suffer from the agony of choice isn't an anomaly; it's one of the most predictable and poignant things about being alive.

Put someone long enough on Earth and they will, through no particular evil quality, tie themselves up in extraordinary knots. They will be assailed by regrets. They will be eaten up every day by the thought that if only they had acted differently a decade before, things would be much better today.

This is a theme to which the Greek tragic writers were highly sympathetic. They thought that the key to dealing with it was to acknowledge a high degree of inevitability of regret. They were particularly taken with the life story of Oedipus. On a journey, the talented and ambitious Oedipus was stopped by people he thought were robbers. He struck out at their leader and killed him. What no one knew at the time was that the man he killed was actually his father. Of course, if this had been clear, everything would have been different. What the Greeks so liked about the story was the sense that it wasn't Oedipus' fault. But much later, when he finds out what he did, he is, of course, tormented by guilt and sorrow.

Adolphe-William Bouguereau, *Orestes Pursued by the Furies*, 1862.
Orestes pursued by "the Furies" of remorse and regret:
an extreme image of a normal experience.

It's a message we benefit from hearing quite often because what helps with regret is the knowledge that every life is burdened by it in some shape or form. The "regret-free life" exists only in songs. The way to diminish regret is to alleviate the sense that one had the option to choose correctly and failed. Disappointment is—as no one in Modernity ever wants to admit—the human condition.

We should go easy on ourselves given that we are living under capitalism. In terms of human experience, it's a new and very complicated way of organizing life. Economists define capitalism in quite technical ways: it means competition between firms for access to investment funds; it means demand is highly mobile, with customers switching from one supplier to another in search of a better deal; it involves a strenuous devotion to innovation, with a constant battle to provide the public with newer and better products at lower prices. In this way, capitalism has brought many good things into people's lives. It has created elegant, exciting cars; delicious sandwiches; charming hotels on remote islands; bright, kindly kindergartens. But, more troublingly, it has also generated some extraordinarily anxious citizens.

In order to face our troubles in a slightly calmer state of mind, we should admit the inherent dignity and complexity of the problem of working out what to do. Rather than follow a Romantic-era faith in intuitive feeling, the process of working out what to do, or what to do next, should be recognized for what it is: one of the most tricky, complicated, and tiring tasks we ever have to undertake. It should be normal to lavish intellectual attention on just this issue. It should be expected that we will, at times, need to seek a great deal of external help. At other points we might need to take a week away from everything and everyone and give ourselves over to solitary thinking, free from the pressures of pleasing (or deliberately confounding) anyone else.

Working out what to do takes all this effort and time not because we are stupid or self-indulgent, but because the decision builds on very imperfect bits of evidence. Confused shards of information are scattered across our experience. What are, in fact, one's strengths? There are moments of boredom, excitement, things we've coped well with, things that have been intriguing for a while and then neglected: all of these need to be located, decoded and interpreted, and pieced together. We have to weigh up certain competing interests. How much risk is one capable of bearing without getting too stressed? How important is it to feel that other people normally respect what you do? Finding accurate answers to these questions means building up a high level of self-knowledge.

One of the most poignant kinds of experience that people develop as they become writers is tolerance of the terrible first draft—and of the second and the third, and maybe many more as well. To someone starting out it seems like a sign of incompetence to produce an initial version that lacks so many of the qualities you'd expect to see in a polished piece of work. There's an expectation that it should be relatively straightforward to string a few decent paragraphs together. The more painful, but productive, insight is that it is actually very tricky to do this. One's thoughts and associations all tumble out of the mind in confused and disordered ways. The thing you want to say is hidden behind a more familiar point. The link between a couple of points isn't at all obvious. You can't tell as yet what should come first and what fits in later. An author might have to redraft the material ten or twenty times before they can understand what it is they are actually trying to say. This is simply how long it takes them to unjumble their ideas. We're not all writing novels, of course, but the sequence of drafts tells us something about the mind in general. There are going to be long, tricky processes involving a lot of crossings-out, a lot of changes and repositioning of material, as we try to understand ourselves.

The big, consequential choices we try to make around career and career development have to be made under inescapably adverse conditions. Often we are short of time; often we don't know enough about the options. Ultimately we are attempting to describe someone we can't possibly fully know—ourselves at a future date— and guess as well as we can what will be best for them. Circumstances will change; whole industries will rise and fall, but we will have built up certain sets of skills, acquired distinctive social connections, fitted ourselves for a future we are only imagining.

We are often exposed primarily to the people in the public realm who have been unusually good at externalizing their talents and acting on their ambitions. By necessity we hear more about these people even though they are in fact pretty rare and, hence, not a reasonable or helpful base for comparison. We would benefit from hearing more about a different range of role models who reveal another, more standard pattern: They cling to mistaken assumptions, take wrong turnings, step carefully away from what later turns out to have been the best option, and commit themselves enthusiastically to disastrous courses of action.

The universal plight is pretty much a sad one. We will almost certainly die with much of our potential undeveloped. Much of what you could have done will remain unexplored. And you may well go to the grave with these parts of yourself pleading for recognition or carrying a sense of failure that there was so much you didn't manage to do. But this isn't really a cause for shame. It ought to be one of the most basic things we recognize about each other: a common fate we face. It's very sad. But it is not sad uniquely to oneself. It is a strangely consoling tragic idea that imagination inevitably outstrips potential. Everyone is unfulfilled; that's a consequence of the odd way our minds have evolved.

The point of this extended tour around the roots of modern experience is to reframe our experience of work, in particular to remind ourselves of how historically elevated our hopes and dreams around employment have been. We're the inheritors of great expectations. These occurred for very noble reasons. But they also carry a grave side effect. It means that we're liable to end up feeling disappointed even in what are, objectively speaking, quite good circumstances. If we can internalize this historical situation, it can help us moderate our hopes in a more realistic direction. Not to depress ourselves (which is how we typically interpret any reduction of hope), but for a far greater reason: to make ourselves feel more cheerful and content.

ii. Self-Compassion

To survive in the modern world, we normally have to get quite good at self-criticism. We make sure that there is nothing our worst enemies could tell us that we have not already fully taken on board: We become experts at the art of self-hatred. We know how to behold our own mediocrity without sentimentality or favor; we allow paranoia to triumph over ease and complacency. Yet so skilled may we become at these maneuvers, our victory is at risk of overshooting. In response to certain professional setbacks, we may grow to despise ourselves to such an extent that we eventually develop difficulties getting out of bed. In time, we may even conclude it might be best just to do away with ourselves.

To attenuate the chances, we should occasionally explore an emotional state of which the ambitious have an understandable tendency to feel extremely scared: self-compassion. Kindness to ourselves can feel like an invitation to indulgence and then disaster, given how much of our success we attribute to anxiety and self-flagellation. But because suicide has problematic aspects too, we should concede the value of calculated moments of self-care.

For a time, until we are stronger, we should be courageous enough to adopt a more generous perspective on ourselves. We may have failed, but we have not thereby forfeited every claim to sympathy and compassion. We were defeated not merely because we were cretins, but also:

1. Because the odds were against us

We fell so readily and heedlessly in love with success, we failed to notice the scale of the challenges we had set ourselves. Without meaning to, we got sucked into the "lottery phenomenon."

In the modern world, many countries have lotteries, and every week many millions of people participate in the hope of suddenly acquiring a substantial fortune. A striking thing is that it's often quite disadvantaged people who are most enthusiastic. We're quite ready to understand how they get the statistics wrong: If they really understood how slim their chances were, they'd never bother. The chances of winning the largest payout is one in 14 million (nearly the same probability as being one of the queen's children, currently a one in 15 million chance). We naturally feel a bit sorry for people investing in such slender hopes. They are taking aim at an impossibly small target.

But we don't notice ourselves doing pretty much the same thing. We too are clutching lottery tickets of various kinds and setting our sights on statistical near-miracles, even though we don't realize we're doing it. And a crucial place where this happens is in our hopes of happiness around work.

Very few people, if any, are truly successful across the whole of a working life. If we were to spell out a picture of the ideally successful career, it might go something like this. Someone early on picks just the right area to apply themselves, discovers and exploits important new opportunities, negotiates excellent contracts, ascends from one high point of achievement to another, swerves neatly into new fields at the ideal moment, gets public recognition and honor for their efforts and retires with the feeling of having accomplished what they set out to do. They enjoy a dignified, respected old age, admired by their descendants and occasionally exercising a deft guiding touch behind the scenes as an *éminence grise*. (They die gently in their 90s of a nonpainful illness in a tranquil, flower-filled room, having written a wise and generous will.)

Such a scenario occurs about as often as a payout at the lottery. But (to our surprise, despite our education and apparently realistic and practical nature) we may have strongly invested imaginatively in some modified version of it: we too think that this is what a good career could look like. And we think that we're not unduly unreasonable if we hope for something like this to happen to us. We don't grasp just how rare and strange a high degree of career success actually is. There are very few places at the top of corporations; very few highly successful entrepreneurs; it's rare for an artist to have commercial success; hardly anyone can make a living from writing novels. And the very few who do succeed in these ways have often paid a high internal cost: relationships have been sacrificed; friendships broken; anxiety levels were high for long periods; they took massive risks that nearly didn't come off; they put in monstrous hours; at times they were driven by manic forces of fear and desperation. We may admire their career achievements but often we wouldn't actually envy the lives they've been living.

Our brains—the faulty walnuts that do our thinking—don't easily understand statistics and probability. We imagine that some things are much more common than they really are. We tend to suppose that the top 1 percent of the population live lives of incredible luxury, flitting round the globe in private jets. But in France the top 1 per cent earn on average around 200,000 euros a year (about $225,000), which is a lot but only enough to buy the wing tip of a Cessna Hemisphere, price tag $30 million. We readily suppose that a lot of people have flat stomachs, though in fact this is extremely unusual: In Australia, for instance, only 2 percent of adults have a slender physique, and by the time one is middle-aged, it is simply freakish to be anything other than flabby. In the UK, about half the population feels worried about money on any particular day; 30 percent of the population feel that no one loves them. But we rarely keep these kinds of facts in mind when we think about our own lives. Instead we are influenced by the images and stories that are more frequently brought to our attention. Without anything sinister lying behind it, the media continually brings anomalies to our notice, because this is what we like to hear about and therefore pay to hear.

Therefore, we feel we're inhabiting a rather different kind of world from the one we actually live in. Our imagined society is likely to contain more murders, more rabid dogs, more man-eating sharks, and more beautiful happy people and more glamorous parties than the real world does. And, of course, we think there are more successful people than there truly are. Our mental map of how much success is likely, probable, normal, or plausible around our careers is inadvertently shifted in an upward direction. Hence we feel less satisfied than we properly should about our own career path.

The data coming into our heads is heavily biased. If we could really see what life and work were like for other people, we'd probably have a very different view of our own attainments and position. If we could fly across the land and peer into everyone's lives and minds like an all-seeing angel, we'd see how very frequent disappointment is; we'd see how much unfulfilled ambition is circulating; how much confusion and uncertainty is being played out in private; how many tears and intemperate arguments there are. We'd get a radically different—and radically more accurate—picture of reality. What we can admit to being is so much more tempered than what we actually are. We'd see how very few people actually make it and we'd see the levels of stress that accompany their outward success. And we'd realize just how abnormal, statistically speaking, the goals we have set ourselves really are.

It would be a painful lesson in some ways. We might be shocked and saddened by what we saw. We'd be disappointed, of course, to conclude that in all probability we won't achieve what we'd hoped to. But in another way, it would be a comforting and reassuring experience.

We'd feel a little more tenderness towards ourselves for not having, in effect, won the job lottery. Instead of fixating on the unrepresentative few, our minds would adjust to the normal ways things tend to go.

Without being overtly naïve, we've probably been blinkered and limited in our ideas about what is likely to happen to us. We've been holding out a hope equivalent to thinking that we might win EuroMillions or the PowerBall jackpot. We don't deserve criticism. We deserve a touch of pity (coming from ourselves) for the formidable obstacles that sit in the way of the kind of career success that we wish we could have and yet is very unlikely to fall to our lot. Our very imperfect working lives come to look less shameful and less distressing when seen, as they should be, against a statistically realistic backdrop.

2. Because we are crazy

With no pejorative intent in mind, just as everyone is and cannot avoid being, we are crazy. We are crazy for only intermittently knowing how to act with reason, for responding to situations through the distorting prisms of our half-forgotten, always troubled childhoods, for failing to understand ourselves or others properly, for losing our grip on our tenuous reserves of patience and equilibrium. This is unavoidable.

The Christian notion of original sin emphasizes that everything human will always, by necessity, be radically imperfect. Our primal ancestors—Adam and Eve—made an error that cast its shadow over the whole of human history. The idea doesn't need to be believed for us to recognize its consoling implications: Our lives have gone wrong not because of this or that mistake on our part but because of a far more profound and basic flaw in our species—an endemic stain that can never be put right.

We inevitably take our craziness along with us in our careers. It's going to mean we will make some rash decisions that work out rather badly. We're going to get furious with certain people who don't actually deserve our ire. We're going to be agitated when we should be calm, and nervous when we need to be confident. We'll end up antagonizing certain people we'd be better off cultivating and be stricken by sloth at moments when we need to focus our efforts. It won't happen all the time—just enough to eat away at our opportunities and to ensure that we don't carve the ideal work path for ourselves. And no matter how much we blame ourselves, these flaws won't go away, because they are not the result of some recent error we're making and could put right. They are part and parcel of our damaged human nature—the quantity of folly we all receive as a reward for simply being born.

3. Because failure is always the more likely outcome

The universal plight is fundamentally a sad one, yet we insist on feeling privately ashamed of what ought to be one of the most basic publicly recognized truths about the human condition: that people fail a lot.

For a long time, our societies have cruelly and sentimentally insisted on the opposite: that we can and will all win. We hear about resilience, bouncing back, never surrendering, and giving it another try. Not all societies and eras have been as merciless. In Ancient Greece, a remarkable possibility—as alien as a trireme to our own era—was envisaged: You could be very good and yet, despite everything, mess up. To keep this idea at the front of the collective imagination, the Ancient Greeks developed the art of tragic drama. Once a year, at huge festivals in the main cities, all the citizens were invited to witness stories of appalling, often grisly, failure: people who had broken a minor law, made a hasty decision, inadvertently slept with the wrong person, and then suffered swift and disproportionate ignominy and punishment. Yet the responsibility was far from belonging to the tragic heroes alone: it was the work of what the Greeks called "fate" or "the Gods"—a poetic way of insisting that destinies do not reasonably reflect the merits of the individuals concerned. We were to leave the theater shorn of easy moralism, sympathetic to the victims, and afraid for ourselves.

Modern societies have a harder time of all this: They appear unable to accept that a truly good person may not succeed. If someone fails, it appears easier for them to believe that they weren't—after all—good in some way, this conclusion defending us against a far more disturbing, less well-publicized, and yet far truer thought: that the world is very unfair.

We all stand on the edge of tragedy, in societies reluctant to offer us sympathetic playwrights to narrate our stories.

4. Because we envy the wrong people

We began to envy them because they seemed so much like us and we wished so ardently to be them. Our sense of a basic equality unleashed competitive agonies. But although from a distance these successful characters did indeed seem very much like us, beneath the surface, they evidently possessed a range of skills we lack: they may have had highly unusual brains adept at synthesizing vast amounts of data in ingenious ways. Or they were driven to work eighteen hours a day or had a ruthless streak that we were fundamentally not capable of or interested in. The haunting thought—why them, why not me?—should no longer invite self-torture and competitive panic, but should edge us towards an unfamiliar feeling of admiration.

There might truly be significant differences between oneself and the envied person. One was never really their equal. It isn't just laziness or some kind of persecutory force that explains our present relative situation. When viewed dispassionately, certain accomplishments are truly beyond us. We should become appreciative spectators, rather than disappointed rivals, of those spectacularly unusual beings who have accomplished great things.

5. Because the macroeconomic picture was wrong

The scope and rewards for particular talents are hugely variable across time. We are creatures of circumstance. How our careers go depends not only on the strength and depth of our own abilities but also on what might be grandly called the epoch of the world.

The ideal is to launch one's interests and talents onto a favorable wave of the economy. Imagine being a competent ecclesiastical architect in the UK in the second half of the 19th century (when there was a long period of exceptionally well-financed church building initiated by many different sects); an OK actor turning up in Hollywood in 1926; or entering the oil industry in 1953, or the mining industry in Australia in 2001, or being a moderately inspired tech entrepreneur in 1997 (who managed to get out in 1999).

These were fabulous times for such careers, although today the prospects are much more restricted. It's not that there's literally no work in these areas, just that it's rare and the competition is ferocious.

In latching onto a career path, one must consider not solely the purely personal question of defining one's abilities and strengths. There's another, totally different, issue in the wings: how favorable the prevailing climate happens to be. Inescapably, we may get caught up in a maelstrom. And those who hit the right seam at the right time were maybe just lucky—although they are often understandably reluctant to admit this.

6. Because we fall foul of office politics

Even if we're in a job that is basically right for us, we're desperately exposed to circumstance in terms of what our colleagues happen to be like. There's always the very real possibility of ending up with imperfect managers, jealous equals, and problematic clients. It's not an accident that we encounter such obstacles to satisfaction at work. It's simply an outcome of a painful fact about people in general: Individuals bring many problems into their working lives. They might be very inept at giving instructions; they might be rendered insecure by the success of others; they might want to dominate in meetings; they could be devious and undermine us behind our backs; or they could have a strong tendency to shift responsibility. The sad thing is that we're very unlikely to be able to find a job where none of this happens, because it's not a failing of particular workplaces so much as a reflection of human nature. The near unavoidability of office politics means that no job is likely to be all that we'd ideally want it to be.

7. Because we are very tired

It feels familiar to attribute our worst panics to solidly grounded facts and ideas. We hit a moment when we feel work is going all wrong. When we mess up or feel we're getting nowhere, we're trained to think that the causes of our troubles must be quite impressive—we've got a mistaken vision of the needs of the job, we lack intelligence, or have blundered into the wrong kind of career. Yet the real explanation of why we feel so low and inept may be only that we haven't had a good breakfast or that we're short of sleep. Perhaps there has been a run of overcast days and we're missing the sunlight; perhaps we've been staring at a screen too long; maybe the air in the office is a bit stale. We imagine we should be looking at drastic remedies—a showdown with a colleague, a dramatic confrontation with a supplier, a curt letter of resignation, or six months of backpacking across the Andes. In fact, what we really need is an early night, a glass of water, a walk around the block or a desktop fan.

It's a move that feels unfamiliar at work. And yet we usually are quite well acquainted with this idea in another area of existence. The generous parent knows, when faced with the tantrums and furies of an infant, that it is not always worth attempting to reason them out of their grief. It may just be the case that one should guide the child to bed and hope very much for a long, restful night. We may need to act as guardians to our own bruised and furious inner child who is not a monster of discontent, but merely suffering from a minor failure of physical comfort.

* * *

Self-compassion is different from saying that we are innocent. It means trying to be extremely understanding around the full range of reasons why people fail. We have been imbeciles, no doubt, but we deserve to exist, to be heard and to be sympathetically forgiven, nevertheless.

iii. Why No Single Job Can Ever Be Enough

We are meant to be monogamous about our work, and yet in any given week, we're likely to spend a good few moments daydreaming of alternatives. We may be paid to rationalize tax payments across three jurisdictions, assess the commercial viability of nail bars in Poland, or help a class of 14-year-olds master quadratic equations; but a part of our brain will for a few moments be taken up with the possible pleasures of managing a ski resort, working in medical research, or operating a travel agency. It's a vagabond tendency that constantly nibbles away at our commitment to our present employment.

We aren't unusually disloyal; we're simply picking up on a fundamental feature of the human condition: We truly have talents in many more job areas than we will ever have the opportunity to explore. Large parts of our working personalities will have to go to the grave unexplored, and therefore make themselves felt in protest before they do so.

We can understand the origins of our restlessness when we look back at our childhoods. As children, we were allowed to do so much. In a single Saturday morning, we might put on an extra sweater and imagine being an Arctic explorer, then have brief stints as an architect making a Lego house, a rock star making up an anthem about cornflakes, and an inventor working out how to speed up coloring in by gluing four felt-tip pens together. We'd put in a few minutes as a member of an emergency rescue team, then we'd try out being a pilot brilliantly landing a cargo plane on the rug in the corridor; we'd perform a life-saving operation on a knitted rabbit and finally we'd find employment as a sous chef helping to make a ham-and-cheese sandwich for lunch.

Each one of these "games" might have been the beginning of a career. And yet we had to settle on only a single option, done repeatedly over fifty years. We are so much more than the world of work ever allows us to be. In his "Song of Myself," published in 1881, the American poet Walt Whitman gave our multiplicity memorable expression: "I am large, I contain multitudes." By this he meant that there are so many interesting, attractive, and viable versions of oneself; so many good ways one could potentially live and work. But very few of these ever get properly played out and become real in the course of the single life we have. No wonder if we're quietly and painfully constantly conscious of our unfulfilled destinies, and at times recognize, with a legitimate sense of agony, that we really could have been something and someone else.

It's not our fault that we have not been able to give our "multitudes" expression. The modern job market gives us no option but to specialize. We cannot be an airline pilot one afternoon a week, a tree surgeon two days a month, and a singer-songwriter in the evenings, while holding down part-time jobs as a political advisor, a plumber, a dress designer, a tennis coach, a travel agent and being, additionally, the owner of a small restaurant serving Lebanese mezze—however much this might be the ideal arrangement to do justice to our widespread interests and potential.

The reasons why we cannot do so much were first elaborated by the Scottish philosopher Adam Smith (1723–1790). In *The Wealth of Nations* (1776), Smith explained how what he termed the division of labor massively increases collective productivity. In a society where everyone does everything, only a small number of shoes, houses, nails, bushels of wheat, horse bridles, and cartwheels are ever produced and no one is especially good at anything. But if people specialize in just one small area (making rivets, shaping spokes, manufacturing rope, bricklaying, etc.) they become much faster and more efficient in their work, and collectively the level of production is greatly increased. By focusing our efforts, we lose out on the enjoyment of multiplicity, yet our society becomes overall far wealthier and better supplied with the goods it needs. It is a tribute to the world Smith foresaw that we have ended up with job titles such as: senior packaging and branding designer, intake and triage clinician, research center manager, risk and internal audit controller and transport policy consultant—in other words, tiny cogs in a giant efficient machine, hugely richer, but full of private longings to give our multitudinous selves expression.

That all of us are doing only a fraction of the work we are temperamentally suited to indicates a whole new way of measuring unemployment. Whatever we may actually be doing, all of us harbor at least nine other employable selves, currently languishing outside the paid job market. In an unfamiliar but real way, the official employment statistics are therefore deeply misleading and far too low. They don't take into account the sheer variety of jobs each person could in principle be doing. There are roughly 33 million people in the UK job market, with 1.69 million officially registered as unemployed at the time of writing—around 5.5 percent. But considered in terms of the multitude of things each person could do, there are in reality around 330 million potential working selves in search of fulfillment at any one time. More than 90 percent of our collective work capacity is underemployed.

Compared to the play of childhood, we are leading fatally restricted lives. There is no easy cure. As Adam Smith argued, the causes don't lie in some personal error we're making: it's a limitation forced upon us by the greater logic of a productive, competitive market economy. But we can allow ourselves to mourn that there will always be large aspects of our character that won't be satisfied. We're not being silly or ungrateful, we're simply registering the clash between the demands of the employment market and the wide-ranging potential of every human life. There's a touch of sadness to this insight. But it is also a reminder that this lack of fulfillment will accompany us whatever we do. It can't be cured by switching jobs. It is an existential sorrow occasioned by the period of history we happen to live in.

There's a parallel here, as so often, between our experience around work and what happens in relationships. It's a strange truth that, given how many people there are in the world, there's no doubt that we could (without any blame attaching to a current partner) have great relationships with dozens, maybe hundreds of different people. They would bring to the fore different sides of our personality, please us (and upset us) in different ways and introduce us to new excitements. Yet, as with work, specialization brings advantages: it means we can focus, bring up children in stable environments, and learn the disciplines of compromise.

In love and work, life requires us to be specialists, even though we are by nature equally suited for wide-ranging exploration. And so we will necessarily carry about within us, in embryonic form, many alluring versions of ourselves that will never be given the proper chance to live. It's a somber thought, but a consoling one too. Our suffering is painful but has a curious dignity to it, because it does not uniquely affect us as individuals. It applies as much to the CEO as to the intern, as much to the artist as to the accountant. Everyone could have found so many versions of happiness that will elude them. In suffering in this way, we are participating in the common human lot. We may with a certain melancholy pride remove the job search engine from our bookmarks and cancel our subscription to a dating site in due recognition of the fact that, whatever we do, parts of our potential will have to go undeveloped and die without having had the chance to come to full maturity, for the sake of the benefits of focus and specialization.

iv. Falling in Love Again

Although it's not a term we normally use, it's entirely possible—common, in fact—to have a crush on a job. It's similar to the way we can have a crush on a person. We see them around (or maybe just catch sight of them once at an airport or in a bar) and think: perhaps with this person I could be happy; the way they do their hair, the kind of shoes they are wearing, the shape of their cheekbones, a particular way of standing or smiling … These little things conjure up a delightful vision of mutual happiness. If we're currently in a relationship, the crush has a powerful tendency to leave us feeling that our present partner isn't all they could be. Maybe we'd be better off ditching them and seeking a newer, more interesting, person to get together with. We're making an unfavorable comparison between the person we know and have become a bit bored by and this new individual whose charms seem so compelling.

Experience usually eventually teaches us to distrust these charming daydreams. But we probably have to make a good few mistakes before we learn the lesson: we discover that the nice shoes didn't actually reveal a calm and poised personality; that the haircut wasn't the outward sign of wit and sparkling intelligence; that the person with the lovely smile could also be mocking and unsympathetic at crucial moments. In other words, we slowly learn that however alluring a person might look on the outside, they will possess the full average quantity of annoying and frustrating qualities (just as we do ourselves).

Something similar goes on around work. We get very excited by the idea of another job. We're acutely sensitive to external indicators and brief descriptions. There's a company that has uncommonly fine offices (polished floors, brick walls, bottles of Evian mineral water); you notice that people in architecture have lovely glasses; someone you meet at a party is going to work for a medical charity in Vanuatu as their logistics director, or a friend of a friend has started a business in luxury stationery and seems to have found a nice niche market. Such starting points are enough for a job-crush to get going. We start building up a fantasy of how great it would be if we were doing these things, and whatever we are actually doing starts to feel unexciting and uninteresting when compared with our mental picture of this other kind of work. We become resentful of our less-than-glamorous colleagues, of our gray office cubicle, of the fact that no one gets envious when we say what we do or that we're still working for other people rather than being our own boss. We used to think we quite liked our work, but a powerful job-crush can make us feel we're badly missing out.

The troubling reality, however, is that every job has problems. It's just that we don't yet have a clear grasp of the tedious, worrying, and upsetting aspects of the job we have a crush on. If we could trial it for a month or two, we'd soon realize. The lovely office belongs to a company with draconian firing policies; two negative reviews in a row and you're out. Someone locked themselves in the bathroom last week in tears. The medical logistics director is continually warding off despair and the insurmountable problems they are trying to deal with. They spend quite a lot of their time negotiating bribes and attempting to minimize the theft of supplies. The luxury paper person is up at three in the morning trying to find a way round their cash-flow problems; and the people with perfect glasses say cruel things behind each other's backs. We're so aware of the problems in our job when we are doing it. Other jobs appear so enticing because we're only exposed to their positive sides. And, additionally, we become deadened to what's actually nice about the work we do—we forget the things that first drew us to it. Its merits drop out of sight, and only its miseries remain clear to us. But with the crush-job all the appealing aspects are still fresh and unfamiliar, and we're immensely alive to them. So it's not really that the other job is much nicer; it's just that the terms of the comparison are unfair to the work we've got.

Rather than be made unhappy by a crush on an imagined job, we should sometimes explore the possibility of learning to fall back in love with the quite-good job we have. We can get involved in the process of reappreciation. It sounds unfamiliar. But actually we've probably encountered reappreciation before. It's a major theme in the arts.

Fields were nice before Monet got around to painting

Claude Monet's *Oat Field Poppies, Giverny* (1890)
gave new glory to a commonplace subject.

them. But farming isn't a very glamorous occupation, and it was unsurprising that many of Monet's contemporaries had forgotten how nice and appealing a field in the countryside could be. Maybe as children they'd liked the idea of strolling through the tall grass, but as adults they associated fields more with mud or cold winter mornings or the unreliable train service from the city. What Monet does is give us a chance to take a second, fresh look at the attractions of fields—at how lovely the colors are, how sweet the blue haze of the distance is, how nice the flowers look among the oats. We get reconnected to charms that were always there but that we'd developed a habit of overlooking.

The same kind of process of positive reacquaintance can occur in relationships. After being together with someone for a few years, their attractions can become familiar and we start to ignore them and become huge experts on all that's annoying and irritating about them. But we sometimes get a chance to reverse the process. It might be that we look at a photo from the time we first got to know them. It reminds us of the really nice things about them that so much excited us at the beginning. We pick up again on their shy smile, on their sympathetic look, on their delightful wrists (shown off by the pushed-back sleeves of a cashmere sweater). Or maybe we go away for a few days to a work conference and, coming back, find they are waiting for us at the airport and our trip has given us just enough psychological distance to appreciate them again. Or we hear that a casual acquaintance has a crush on our partner and thinks they are fascinating and elegant. Mixed in with a dose of irritation, we can also have a very interesting rediscovery: Via this potential rival's eye, we see again what it is we could conceivably lose.

In other words, we are adaptable creatures. Disenchantment is not a one-way street. We can sometimes reverse the direction. We are capable of a second, more accurate look. We can perform a Monet-type move around our own work. Ideally we'd have a great artist train their sights on our working day and pick out just what is lovely and appealing about it and show it to us— we'd be able to buy the postcard and pin it above our desks. But failing that, we can perform a version of the same operation ourselves.

We could suppose that someone was interviewing us about our career and asked: What are the three best things about your job? What would the answers be? It won't be surprising, of course. But it will redirect our attention to the genuine positives that are there, but that don't occupy the front of our minds day to day. Or suppose a magazine was doing a photoshoot in our workplace with the specific brief to make it look interesting and exciting: what shots might they take? It's like the way a selling agent can take shots of a house that deeply surprise the owners and make them feel they'd forgotten just what a nice home they actually have and are now, perhaps stupidly, in the process of moving out of.

We can teach ourselves to fall back in love, to some extent, with our current work. It won't be infatuation. It won't be like the first time we fall in love when we believe that another person (or job) will be ideal. It will be a more mature, but still real, kind of love, that's well aware of the imperfections and flaws, that's conscious of compromise and areas of difficulty, but still feels real warmth and appreciation for the important merits that are genuinely there. It's similar to what can happen in a relationship, when after perhaps years of feuding and frustration a couple starts to take a more measured view of one another. They know this isn't what they dreamed of. But they can see that the other person is very largely on their side and truly wants what's best for them. Even if it's not exactly what the other would want for themselves, the good will is real. Their less dramatic virtues can be acknowledged and the quieter pleasures of being together appreciated.

Falling back in love with a job means that we understand the error of the job-crush. We've come to admit that no job can be everything one might want, but it can still have much that we can take pride and pleasure in.

v. Good-Enough Work

It sounds a bit awful to tell others (or ourselves) not to aim too high. It can come across as sour and defeatist. Sometimes, of course, it is just that. But at other points, it can be deeply wise and generous advice, because it combats the strange and powerful way we have of unfairly attacking ourselves for not living up to imagined ideals.

This move of undercutting our reckless perfectionism was first developed by the British psychoanalyst Donald Winnicott in the 1950s. Winnicott specialized in relationships between parents and children. In his clinical practice, he often met with parents who were trying their best to be everything to their children and yet were in despair. The parents were angry and frustrated at how far from their ideals their family lives were turning out to be: the children might be withdrawn or naughty, the parents might be tired and irritable. Hopes had often curdled into desperate frustration.

Winnicott's crucial insight was that the parents' agony was coming from a particular place: They were trying too hard. To help them, he developed a charming and highly practical concept of what he called "the good-enough parent." Children, he insisted, don't need an ideal parent. They very much need an OK, pretty decent, usually well-intentioned, and generally, but not always, warm and reasonable father or mother. This wasn't because Winnicott liked to settle for second best, but rather because he realized that, in order to become well-balanced, robust, and enduring souls (a very big ambition in reality), we need to cope with imperfection and resist torturing ourselves trying to be what no ordinary human can be.

The concept of "good enough" was invented to give dignity to a failure to live up to a punishing, counter-productive ideal. It pointed out that much that is really important goes on at a much lower level than the flawless and problem-free. Winnicott was trying to tell parents that "good enough" is a saner and therefore more honorable goal.

With Winnicott's advice to parents in mind, we could usefully develop the notion of a good-enough job. A good-enough job has the normal, full range of defects: it's a bit boring at some points; it has fiddly, frustrating aspects; it involves times of anxiety; you have to put up with occasionally being judged by people you don't especially respect; it doesn't perfectly utilize all your merits; you are never going to make a fortune; sometimes you have to cut corners when you'd rather not; you have to be polite to some rather irritating people; your best ideas won't always get taken up; certain rivals will in all probability surpass you; and there will be days when you wonder how you could have been such an idiot as to get involved in this in the first place.

But, in a good-enough job, along the way there will be plenty of positive aspects. You'll make some close friends; you'll have times of real excitement; you'll quite often see that your best efforts are recognized and rewarded; you'll appreciate the overall worthwhile direction of what you and the rest of the team are doing; you'll finish many days tired but with a sense of accomplishment.

The public probably won't be singing your praises; you won't get to the very top; you won't singlehandedly change the world; many of the early fantasies of what a career might be will gently drop aside. But you will know that you work with honor and dignity and that, in a quiet, mature, non-starry-eyed but very real way, *you love your job enough*. And that is, in itself, a very grand achievement.

Picture Credits

Also available from The School of Life:

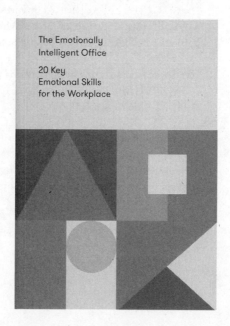

The Emotionally
Intelligent Office

20 Key
Emotional Skills
for the Workplace

The Emotionally Intelligent Office

20 key emotional skills for the workplace

An in-depth exploration of what lies behind our problematic behavioral patterns in the workplace, and a blueprint for the emotional skills we need to overcome them.

Stress and mental ill health currently costs the US economy upwards of $300 billion a year. Modern businesses continue to place huge emphasis on technical training, yet a lot of what determines the success or failure of organizations has nothing to do with the sort of hard skills taught at business school; instead, it comes down to the degree of emotional intelligence circulating in the workplace.

This is a book that introduces us to twenty core emotional skills that can help businesses to flourish. They range from giving honest feedback, to accepting that it's OK to fail, to addressing jealousies and insecurities within teams. We learn about how our childhoods continue to have an often unhelpful impact on how we deal with colleagues, and the best ways we might speak so that others will listen.

ISBN: 978-0-9957535-8-7
£12 | $16.99

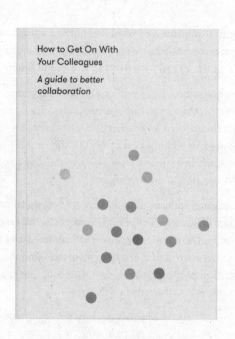

How to Get On With
Your Colleagues

*A guide to better
collaboration*

How to Get on With Your Colleagues

A guide to better collaboration

An essential guide to navigating the complexities of professional relationships in the office.

The most difficult aspect of work has nothing to do with profitability or deadlines or competition. It has to do with the immense and beautiful challenges opened up by the fact that we must deal, on an ongoing basis, with that often amazing but always complicated entity known as the colleague.

Our colleagues can be the sources of our greatest joys and triumphs: They compensate for our weaknesses, enlarge our strengths, and aggregate our energies. However, working successfully around others is neither intuitive nor simple: It requires us to communicate effectively, to understand our own minds and blind spots, to master our emotions, and to see the world through others' perspectives.

The School of Life has been working with organizations since its foundation. This book compresses our learning into a series of lessons on workplace psychology. The result is an essential guide to more profitable, harmonious, and happier organizations.

ISBN: 978-1-912891-15-3

£10 | $14.99

How to Think
More Effectively

A guide to greater
productivity, insight
and creativity

How to Think More Effectively

A guide to greater productivity, insight, and creativity

A guide to identifying, nurturing, and growing our insight and creativity for more effective thinking.

We know that our minds are capable of great things because, every now and then, they come out with a brilliant idea or two. However, our minds are also unpredictable, spending large stretches of time idling or distracting themselves. This is a book about how to optimize these beautiful yet fitful instruments so that they can more regularly and generously produce the sort of insights and ideas we need to fulfill our potential and achieve the contentment we deserve. Among other things, we learn how to grasp fragile and flighty thoughts before they disappear through anxiety and fear; at what times of day to try to work and for how long; how to make use of our boredom and instincts; and how to overcome timid and predictable approaches to the largest problems. The result is an operating manual to that most wondrous, though intermittent and always baffling, organ: the human mind.

ISBN: 978-1-912891-13-9

£10 | $14.99

THE SCHOOL OF LIFE

On
Failure

How to succeed at defeat

The School of Life: On Failure

How to succeed at defeat

**A reassuring guide on how to overcome failure,
teaching us that we can learn to fail well.**

This is a hopeful, consoling, gentle book about failure. Our societies talk a lot about success, but the reality is that no one gets through life without failing—in small and usually also in large ways. Sometimes our failures are very obvious; at other times, we feel we have to conceal them out of shame. This book encourages us to accept the role that failure plays for all of us and to feel compassion for ourselves for the messes we can't help but make as we go through our lives.

This is a book packed with dignified, sensible, kindly suggestions about how to approach failure: how to deal with friends, how to cope with enemies, how to endure regret, how to pick ourselves up, how to accept ourselves despite our flaws—and how to endure and thrive in new, less than ideal circumstances.

When we fail, it can sometimes seem as if failure is freakish and out of the ordinary. In truth, there is nothing more human than failure—and nothing wiser and more necessary than to learn to fail well.

ISBN: 978-1-912891-67-2

£16 | $21.99

The School of Life publishes a range of books on essential topics in psychological and emotional life, including relationships, parenting, friendship, careers, and fulfillment. The aim is always to help us to understand ourselves better—and thereby to grow calmer, less confused, and more purposeful. Discover our full range of titles, including books for children, here:

www.theschooloflife.com/books

The School of Life also offers a comprehensive therapy service, which complements, and draws upon, our published works:

www.theschooloflife.com/therapy